MICROBE BASE MANUAL
Apple® II +, IIc & IIe version

JOHN MAGEE
Department of Microbiology
The Children's Hospital
Sheffield
England

PHILIP WHEAT
Department of Bacteriology
Royal Hallamshire Hospital
Sheffield
England

1985

ACADEMIC PRESS
(Harcourt Brace Jovanovich, Publishers)
London   Orlando   San Diego   New York
Toronto   Montreal   Sydney   Tokyo

ACADEMIC PRESS INC. (LONDON) LTD.
24/28 Oval Road,
London NW1 7DX

United States Edition Published by
ACADEMIC PRESS INC.
(Harcourt Brace Jovanovich, Inc.)
Orlando, Florida 32887

ISBN 0-12-465016-3

Printed in Great Britain

PREFACE

This manual and the associated programs are primarily for use in diagnostic microbiology laboratories, but we hope that they will also find non-medical applications. We have recognised for many years the value of analysing laboratory records, but are also familiar with the tedium and manpower costs involved in searching paper records. The programs have been used for several years by our colleagues and ourselves, vindicating our belief in record analysis, and relieving the tedium involved. During this time some impressions have proved false and others have been affirmed by the availability of accurate statistics. It is our hope that the programs will be equally effective in other hospitals and other contexts. If these establishments should discover novel applications of the programs, we would be pleased to hear of them. The programs have found research applications in our hands and, again, we would be pleased to see credit given should others publish data derived from their use.

The programs and manual could not have been published without the patience, assistance and advice of many people. We are pleased to acknowledge the help of our colleagues in the diagnostic laboratories of southern Sheffield, friends from other laboratories, our publishers and, particularly, of our families.

CONTENTS

INTRODUCTION

The Problem

The records of antibiotic susceptibility patterns and species isolated retained by a diagnostic microbiology laboratory contain a wealth of information relevant to local trends in antimicrobial susceptibility, epidemiological patterns and cross infection. These records are kept in paper form by the majority of laboratories and may contain details for between 2,000 and 15,000 isolates pa. The amount of information entering these records tends to increase each year as workloads rise, more antimicrobials are tested, or more detailed identification is undertaken. The recent rise of breakpoint and multipoint inoculation methods suited to the 'mass production' of susceptibility and identification information reflect this trend, although MICROBE BASE does not depend upon use of these techniques. A minority of the largest laboratories have computerised records and reporting systems to deal with vast workloads and some of these incorporate search facilities. These use very expensive mini- or main frame computers. However the average hospital laboratory has not seen any parallel advance in methods of coping with the analysis of isolate information.

Rising workloads mean that analysis for epidemiological, susceptibility and cross infection purposes is becoming more relevant and rewarding, but, paradoxically, much more difficult to carry out because of the sheer weight of information. Manual recovery of information on specific patients or specimens is usually simple and rapid, but the more general perspective of local trends is lost or has to rely upon current impressions rather than accurate information. It can be very expensive, tedious and morale destroying to attempt to carry out even quite simple, appropriate analyses and the process can be so time consuming as to give results which are only of historical relevance. The accuracy of the analysis depends heavily upon the diligence and cooperation of staff who are employed for their scientific ability rather than to carry out clerical tasks. Current financial stringencies and workloads mean that regular review of trends and pursuing leads, which can add so much interest to the work, are almost impossible. In effect potentially valuable information is lost to the laboratory for lack of a cost effective analysis system.

The Solution

In recent years the price of the microcomputer has fallen to the point where it is within the range of non-capital expenditure for most laboratories; indeed many laboratory staff own a home computer and so are familiar with their use. MICROBE BASE is designed to be a cost effective solution to the problems of analysis of susceptibility information, working on an inexpensive microcomputer systems, and requiring a minimum of staff time in training and routine use. The MICROBE BASE software was written and developed by microbiologists who work in a diagnostic laboratory and are familiar not only with the problem, but also with the capabilities, skills and attitudes of staff, and the variation of patterns of work between laboratories.

MICROBE BASE is designed to be simple to operate, taking the user through a logical sequence of screen instructions and menus, with checking routines which ensure that the typing errors of the inexperienced user are ignored. The user need not be familiar with programming, and soon becomes conversant with the computer keyboard. MICROBE BASE can be readily incorporated into the routine of the laboratory without any need for extra staff, and entry of a day's results for a large district general hospital - details on about 45 isolates - takes only 10-20 minutes. Analysis of the information on 9,600 isolates using the system takes less than 5 minutes of user time and about 60 minutes of computer time, including printing of the results; we have found that this is a realistic time scale for almost all queries. All the information recorded using MICROBE BASE is protected from unauthorised access by a password system, and is held in duplicate on a PRIME and BACKUP data disk in case of accidental damage to a disk. Use of this program does not monopolise the computer's time, leaving the system free for other uses such as word processing, label printing and program development.

What information goes in?

MICROBE BASE is primarily designed to record details relevant to susceptibility, epidemiology and cross infection information, but there could be considerable flexibility in its use; other potential applications are discussed below. For the primary purpose, however, the information required on each isolate entered is laboratory number, site or type of specimen, ward or department, consultant, species or genus, and a susceptibility pattern for up to 11 antibiotics. The information recorded is protected against unauthorised access or entry by a password security system, and against accidental loss or damage by a duplicate backup system.

What are the benefits and applications?

One of the major benefits that can be derived very quickly from use of MICROBE BASE is that the laboratory will be seen to be actively monitoring significant local isolates down to levels as fine as ward/department and consultant. This awareness can have quite significant effects alone. The laboratory can give details of CURRENT LOCAL susceptibility patterns, rather than relying upon impressions, publications from other hospitals or the literature of the pharmaceutical industry. Particular departments, such as Intensive Care or Special Care Baby Units can be monitored on a monthly or even weekly basis. Guidelines on current susceptibility patterns in particular situations can be issued to the relevant clinicians, e.g. for urines from general practice or ante-natal clinics. The status of current hospital epidemiology can be assessed by an organism audit, problem areas identified, and the efficacy of solutions monitored by regular epidemiological analysis. The history of cross infection incidents can be rapidly tracked down. The simplicity of computer assisted analysis allows such searches to be carried out at a much lower level of suspicion, and therefore much more frequently than with manual systems. This means that outbreaks could be detected at a much earlier stage. There are potential uses in quality control of susceptibility testing and primary isolation, involving monitoring of overall sensitivity and isolation rates. Possible research uses include comparative analysis of susceptibilities to new agents. Managerial uses might include recovery of accurate figures for work generated by individual wards/departments as a result of positive cultures or calculation of the revenue consequences of the introduction of new clinical units. In effect access to information on every significant isolate is possible. This list is not exhaustive; ingenuity and knowledge of the problems of an individual unit will suggest other potential uses.

Flexibility of MICROBE BASE

The search and summary facilities are very flexible. The programs are based on the concept of a user defined description file, and can therefore be adapted to the pattern of work in each laboratory. For example, if the majority of _Enterobacteriacea_ isolates are identified to species level then the user defined list might include all the more common species individually, and the less common as groups, e.g. _Serratia_ _spp_. Another laboratory might carry out little identification of such organisms, and be happy to employ groups such as coliform, _Proteus_ _spp_. etc. Similar considerations apply to specimen site. If the laboratory wishes to differentiate between mid stream and catheter urines, surgical and accidental wounds or blood cultures from diabetics, leukemics and others then the user need only specify a suitable range of specimen site codes. Similarly although susceptibilities for up to 11 agents can be recorded, for many species only a few agents might be specified. Indeed, the dummy data supplied for training includes records of virus and parasite isolations, for which no susceptibilities are recorded. For certain types of specimen and organism a laboratory may test more than 11 agents; in this case the user must choose which results are to be recorded. So the user can determine how much detail enters the records. It is quite certain that each laboratory will have its own unique version of the description file, and therefore its own individually tailored system.

The program used to design and record description files include routines for transferring these files to and from the program disk. This means that a laboratory can run more than one version of the programs. An example here might be a general sensitivity records system for the laboratory, plus a separate system for recording results from a venereal diseases clinic. The programs can be used in other ways, for example a culture collection list could be held with the specimen site, ward and consultant codes actually recording source of isolate, laboratory number recording the culture designation, and the 11 antibiotic spaces used to record biochemical reactions, or suitable storage and recovery media and culture intervals. A version for a special care baby unit might record results for individual patients, rather than wards. A version for a venereal disease clinic might record postcodes rather than consultant, or an enviromental control version might use the SENS columns to represent numbers isolated - the first column as 10^1 , the second as 10^2 and so on. The headings used to describe the information recorded are not intended to bind the user; a little ingenuity will usually allow MICROBE BASE to be applied to other microbiological information storage and retrieval problems.

MICROBE BASE was developed as a result of the proven practical value of a set of programs, which were constructed for use by experts in one particular laboratory. The programs are now designed to be as flexible as the computer system will allow, and are suited to use by any laboratory, whatever the level of computer expertise and knowledge. The minimum Apple system required to operate the programs costs $1200-$1500. Consumable stores expenditure for paper, printer ribbons and disks is likely to be less than $60 p.a. The system should be a useful and cost effective asset in your efforts to improve the standard of patient care in your hospital.

The remainder of this manual consists of four chapters of familiarisation exercises, and a reference section. The exercises are intended to familiarise your staff with the operation of MICROBE BASE using a dummy information base designed around a fictitious laboratory. These chapters were written in a progression from the most to least used portions of the programs. It is MOST IMPORTANT that any potential user reads the section on Precautions and Advice before attempting the familiarisation exercises.

LEARNING TO USE THE PROGRAMS

The three floppy disks supplied with this manual are labelled PROGRAMS, PRIME DATA, and BACKUP DATA. The PROGRAMS disk contains the MICROBE BASE programs, and an information list describing a fictitious hospital. The organisation of this description list is shown in Appendix 1. Although this consists of 15 pages of information describing a large organisation, it is essentially repetitive and simple. The PRIME DATA disk contains details of 2000 organisms isolated at this hospital, and the BACKUP DATA disk is an exact copy of this. These disks are included so that the facilities of MICROBE BASE can be demonstrated in the exercises using dummy data.

The second part of this manual is divided into four further chapters, DATA INPUT, ANALYSIS, DISK UTILITIES and DESCRIPTION LISTS. Each of these chapters outlines a series of exercises intended to be carried out using the dummy data supplied with the package. It is recommended that the user should work through the first three of these chapters. Once familiar with the programs one should read the chapter on description lists. This gives details of how to preserve the description list for the fictitious data supplied in the package for later teaching, and how to set up a description list for the user's hospital. Careful thought and planning of the description list at this stage will save the effort required for later piecemeal amendment. Enter, record and backup the new description list as described in the fourth chapter, and then go ahead with recording and analysing your own information. Several examples of useful analyses are given in the appropriate sections, but these are not exhaustive. The emphasis is on flexibility and the current users have not examined all the possibilities involved.

Once one is familiar with the programs and a routine has been established to enter data there

should be very few problems, most of which can be
solved by use of the Reference Section. However
major problems will arise if the operators ignore
the rules for handling disks described in
Precautions and Advice and emphasis on this is
advised.

PRECAUTIONS AND ADVICE

Computer and Keyboard

DO NOT press CTRL+RESET when the programs are running.

The SHIFT, OPEN- and CLOSED-APPLE and CTRL keys should NOT be pressed when the programs request the user to press any key.

The computer will occasionally 'freeze', giving no apparent activity on the screen or response to keypresses. It is performing 'housekeeping' functions and may not unfreeze for about a minute. DO NOT press keys at random, since the program will store the keypresses and try to interpret them when it unfreezes. This is very rare on most routines except those involved in description file modification.

The convention adopted in this manual, and in the program instructions is to represent a keypress by printing the symbols on the face of the key eg **RETURN** or **C.** These keypresses may be displayed in lower case on the screen, so for example, pressing C may print a lower case c on the screen. The manual occasionally asks the user to hold down SHIFT and press a letter key, which will result in a capital letter being displayed, just as on a typewriter.

Disks and Drive

Note that disks are easily damaged. DO NOT touch or otherwise contaminate the recording surface of the disk. DO NOT bend disks, or place them in a strong magnetic field or write on them with ballpoint pens or pencils. Always store disks in their envelopes when they are not in the drive, preferably in a box which will protect them from direct sunlight and extremes of temperature and humidity.

Use single sided, double density, soft sectored 5 3/4" floppy disks.

The disks must be inserted into the drive slot with the label side up, read window towards the drive and write protect notch to the right of the user.

Regular maintainance of drives is essential.

Printer

If the computer requests that the printer be connected ensure that the printer is on, connected to the computer, and has sufficient paper, correctly inserted and free to feed through. The printer interface must be plugged into slot 1.

Power Supply

A reliable power supply is required for the hardware. Power fluctuations may erase the memory of the computer or drive and lead to intermittent malfunctions in the programs. Various commercial devices are available which can be fitted to the power input line. These will smooth out minor fluctuations. Power failures will erase the current program from the computer memory, requiring reloading from the programs disk.

Emergency Shutdown

To stop the programs in extreme emergency press CTRL+RESET to restart the system, then enter an invalid password to exit. Remove the disk and switch off the computer and printer.

ENTERING INFORMATION

This chapter describes how to load the programs, how to access the 'Help' facilities, what 'Help' facilities are available, entry of information on significant isolates and recording this onto disk.

GETTING STARTED:-

Set up the computer system as described in the manufacturer's manuals. Insert the programs disk in the drive then switch on the printer, computer and television in that order. If you have two disk drives you should always use drive 1 unless otherwise instructed. Copyright information is displayed, then the program asks for a valid password.

MICROBE BASE

ENTER YOUR OPERATOR CODE

This is the security routine which prevents non-operators from gaining access to the stored information or adding invalid information. The only operator code on the dummy data description list is JTM. Press **J** and look at the screen; the J is not displayed so unauthorised users cannot see the password. An X is printed to acknowledge that a keypress has been made. Now press **T** then **M.** The drive operates, a 'Loading Data' message appears and then the screen displays a master menu.

MICROBE BASE

Options Available:-

1) Enter susceptibility information

2) Recover information

3) Use summary routines

4) Use disk handling routines

5) Set up/alter description list

6) End program

Press a number (1-6)

Press the **A** key. The computer is expecting a number. When a letter key is pressed it replies with an error message to tell the operator that the keypress was invalid, then ignores the keypress and continues to wait for a valid number. The error message on the Apple versions consists of an audio beep.

This process of screening the information entered at the keyboard is called input validation. Even the most experienced computer operators make entry errors, so MICROBE BASE examines every keypress to ensure that it makes sense. The program cannot ensure that an entry is correct, i.e. what was meant, but it can filter out the majority of errors by comparing the keys pressed to a list of 'allowed' keypresses and rejecting entries not on the list. This is the operator's safety net, and is a feature of all entry operations on MICROBE BASE.

The first exercises concern the entry of information. Press **1**. If there is no disk in the drive, the wrong disk, or the drive is malfunctioning an appropriate error message is displayed and the operator is allowed to rectify the error.

In normal circumstances the screen displays the MICROBE BASE logo and the message 'PLEASE WAIT, LOADING ENTRY PROGRAM', then, after a period clears again and displays message:-

```
              SENSITIVITY ROUTINES

        Place prime records disk in drive
             Close the drive door


          Press C to continue, E to end
```

The PROGRAMS disk should be removed from the drive and the PRIME DATA disk should be inserted in its place. Then press **C** and the program will check that the correct disk has been inserted. If not then an error message will be displayed asking the user to replace the incorrect disk. Otherwise an input request is displayed.

```
            ENTER WEEK NUMBER   *
```

The number of the current week in the year is being requested. January 1-7th is week 1, 8-14 is week 2 and so on to week 52 at the end of December. The Program Log on the first page of the Appendix shows that the last entry was made at the start of week 8 so enter the week number **8,** then press **RETURN.**

This routine is intended to make the user take note of the date and to keep a paper record of the dates corresponding to the computer generated entry numbers. It was intended that the programs should record this, but the routines consumed too much processing time and memory. A set of log sheets similar to those in the Appendix kept as a manual record is the cost effective solution.

After validation checks the computer, assured that an authorised operator is answering and the correct data disk is in the drive, will allow information to be entered.

```
           SENSITIVITY INPUT ROUTINES

         Hit ^ to record * for help
              Enter data now
  CN (XX)LNO    WRD  CON  SPP       SENS  XXX
  2001  *
```

This is the standard format in which records are
presented on the screen. There is a title line,
which tells the operator which routine is being
used. Below this there are 1 or 2 operator
instruction lines, which give instructions on how
to move on to the next display. Below this is the
header line, which gives a title to each column of
information. Going through these titles in order,
CN is the computer reference number for the entry
on that line. This is assigned automatically by the
computer and cannot be altered by the operator. The
entries are numbered sequentially from 1 to 96000
in order of entry for each data disk. The column
headed LNO contains a code indicating the type or
site of specimen, followed by a laboratory
reference number of up to 5 digits. The next
column, headed WRD, contains 3 letter abbreviations
indicating the ward or department of origin, eg mog

might indicate Medical Out Patients at the General Hospital, or 2ap ward 2A at the Paediatric Hospital. The heading CON indicates that the three letter abbreviations in the next column refer to the consultant in charge of the patient. The three letter abbreviations in the next column, headed SPP, indicate the species and the 11 characters in the next column headed SENS indicate the susceptibility of the organism to 11 agents.

The codes and abbreviations used in entering information are specified by the user in a DESCRIPTION LIST. This is generated by use of the description list writer program whose workings are described in a later section. In these exercises the description list for a hypothetical laboratory serving a district general hospital, burns unit and paediatric hospital is being used. The codes and abbreviations specified by this list are documented in the Appendix.

'HELP' Facilities:-

The 'Help' facilities are accessed by pressing * when the cursor is on the left of the LNO column. Press * and the screen clears and presents a menu.

```
              SENSITIVITY INPUT ROUTINES


Would you like:-

1) Instructions

2) Tables of valid data

3) Return to entry tables


Press the appropriate number (1-3)
```

These 'HELP' facilities are intended to assist with instructions or remind the user of the less commonly used codes in the description list. The

'Instructions' option allows access to 5   pages   of
instructions condensed from this manual.   Press   **1.**
The screen clears and then displays:-

Place programs disk in drive
Close the drive door

Press C to continue, E to end

    Try inserting the wrong disk or even no disk   at
all. Then press **C.** The   computer   will   display   an
appropriate error message and request insertion   of
the correct disk. This is a safety feature designed
to avoid problems caused by the occasional lapse in
concentration. The authors   prompt   these   messages
quite regularly.
    When the correct   disk   has   been   inserted   the
first page of user instructions will be displayed.

> When the computer is turned off, start
> Microbe Base as follows: insert the
> PROGRAMS disk in drive 1, close
> the drive door, and switch the computer
> on. Microbe Base will then start
> automatically. If the power is
> already on, you can start or re-start
> the program by inserting the PROGRAMS
> disk and pressing the Open-Apple, CTRL
> and RESET keys simultaneously. The
> computer will request a valid 3-letter
> operator code before allowing access to
> the routines.
>
> In all routines, the user will be
> informed of errors by a beep, sometimes
> accompanied by an error message. A
> beep does not always mean an error; it
> is sometimes used just to alert the
> user to an unusual condition.
>
> Press C to continue, E end,

Press C for each next page or E to end. When the
final message requests the user to do so, replace
the PRIME DATA disk in the drive and press **C** to
continue. The display reverts to the menu giving a
choice of 'Instructions', 'Valid   entries'   or
'Return to entry table'.

```
            SENSITIVITY INPUT ROUTINES


Would you like:-

1) Instructions

2) Tables of valid data

3) Return to entry tables


Press the appropriate number (1-3)
```

To explore the other 'HELP' facility - 'Valid data' press **2,** and the valid data menu is displayed.

```
            SENSITIVITY INPUT ROUTINES


Would you like to see the valid data
list for:-


1) Specimen type codes

2) Wards

3) Consultants

4) Species

5) Return to entry table


Press the appropriate number (1-5)
```

This allows access to the information in the

description list - in other words the entries which the computer has been told to recognise as acceptable.

First press **1** to examine the acceptable specimen site codes which have been specified by the user for this hospital. These are detailed in the Appendix for comparison. Press **C** and the computer reverts to the valid entry menu. Press **2** to review the valid ward codes, then press **C** to revert to the menu. Press **3** to review the valid consultant codes, then **C** for the menu.

Now to review the valid species list press **4.** The first page of data allows entry of an unlisted or unknown organism. Press **C** for the first defined entry data.

```
              VALID BACTERIA DATA


   Species   1              S.aureus
   One character code       s
   Three letter code        sau

   Antibiotic 1             Penicillin
   Antibiotic 2             Fluclox
   Antibiotic 3             Fusidic acid
   Antibiotic 4             Gentamicin
   Antibiotic 5             Chloramphen
   Antibiotic 6             Tetracycline
   Antibiotic 7             Vancomycin
   Antibiotic 8             Clindamycin
   Antibiotic 9             Erythromycin
   Antibiotic 10            Trial 1
   Antibiotic 11            Trial 2

          Press C to continue, E to end
```

This display introduces some important concepts. Each species code has an associated list of 11 antimicrobial drugs defining the drug referred to for each of the 11 positions in the SENS column. The list of antimicrobials may vary between species. In this case 11 antibiotics are specified, including two antibiotics on in vitro trial. Each species can be entered as either a one letter code or a three letter code. The three letter codes can be devised in a logical fashion. The fictitious laboratory has used the first letter of the generic name followed by the first two letters of the specific name for most species so that the code can be deduced quite simply by the operator. Single letter codes cannot be assigned in such a logical fashion, and so will probably only be remembered readily for the most common species; however a single letter code can be entered more rapidly. This one or three letter code entry system allows the user both speed of entry for the most common species and a logical code system for the less common types.

   To review all the species data simply press **C** for each new page or press **E** to return to the valid data menu.

   In these exercises the 'Help' facilities and the valid code lists in the Appendix can be used. When the user has defined a description list for his own laboratory the codes will be accessible via the 'Help' facilities and valid code lists can be printed out via the description list writer program.

Entry of Susceptibility Information

   To exit from the 'Help' facilities return to the valid data menu and press **5.** The screen reverts to the entry table so:-

```
             SENSITIVITY INPUT ROUTINES

          Hit ^ to record * for help
               Enter data now
  CN    LNO   WRD   CON   SPP       SENS
  2001  *
```

To recapitulate, there is a title line, telling
the operator which routine is being used and 1 or 2
operator instruction lines, giving instructions on
how to move on. Below this is the header line,
giving a title to each column of information. Going
through these in order, CN is the computer
reference number for the entry on that line. This
is assigned automatically by the computer and
cannot be altered by the operator. The entries are
numbered sequentially from 1 to 9,600 in order of
entry for each data disk. The column headed LNO
contains the code indicating the type or site of
specimen, followed by a laboratory reference number
of up to 5 digits. The next column, headed WRD,
contains 3 letter codes indicating the ward or
department of origin. The next column, headed CON,
contains three letter codes indicating the

consultant in charge of the patient. The three
letter codes in the next column, headed SPP,
indicate the species of the organism and the 11
characters in the next column headed SENS indicate
the antibiotic susceptibility of the organism.

The codes and abbreviations used in entering
information are specified by the description list
which you have just reviewed.
Some special function keys are used in the next
sections, which differ between the various Apple
keyboards. To assist the user the Apple IIc/IIe
keypresses are given in the text, followed by the
equivalent keypress for the Apple II+ enclosed in
square brackets eg [CTRL+A]. These differences are
tabulated below and on the quick reference card.

FUNCTION	IIe/IIc	II+
Delete previous character	DEL	←
Non-destructive backspace	←	CTRL+A
Cursor right	→	→ or CTRL+S
Delete species entry	open-apple+DEL	CTRL+X

The program has assigned the computer reference
number 2001 to the next entry, because the PRIME
data disk supplied with the package already has
details of 2000 dummy isolates. The cursor, a
flashing * symbol, is in the first position of the
laboratory number column, and so is awaiting a
valid specimen site code. Press **W**, which indicates
that the specimen is a wound swab. A w is printed
and the cursor moves to the next space.

The next 5 spaces are reserved for a laboratory
number. Enter the number **99999**. Notice that the
number has been printed and, because it is a 5
digit number the cursor has automatically moved to
the first position of the 'WRD' column.

Press the **DEL** key [←] to tell the computer that the last entry was incorrect. The cursor moves back.

Now enter the number **1Ø28.** This leaves the cursor in the last position of the LNO column, since the computer does not know that the entry is complete.

Press **RETURN** to indicate completion of a LNO entry consisting of less than 5 digits. The cursor now moves to the WRD column.

Type in **QQQ.** The letters are printed on the screen, but they do not correspond to a hospital ward in the description list, so the validation check made when all 3 characters have been entered finds that the entry is invalid. The entry is erased, a beep warns the operator and the cursor returns to the start of the WRD column.

Now type in **5D** then press **DEL** [←] because the D was entered in error and should have been an A. The d is deleted.

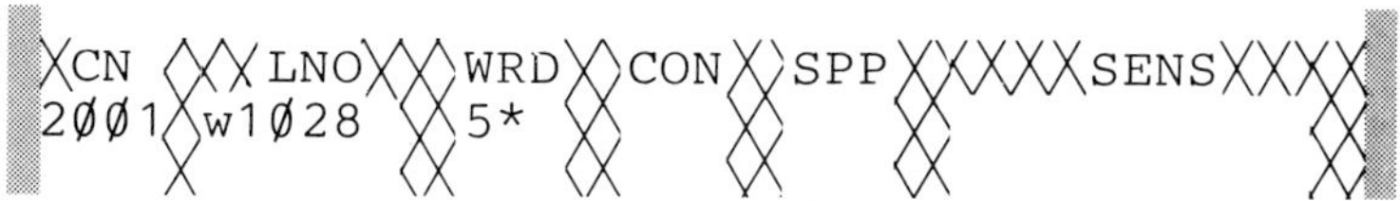

Complete the entry by typing **AG.** This completes 5ag - the code for ward 5A at the general hospital in the description list. The check indicates a valid entry, and the cursor moves to the next column.

The consultant in charge of the case is S.A.Williams, and the entry in the CON column is his initials, **SAW.** Type this and the computer accepts it as a valid entry.

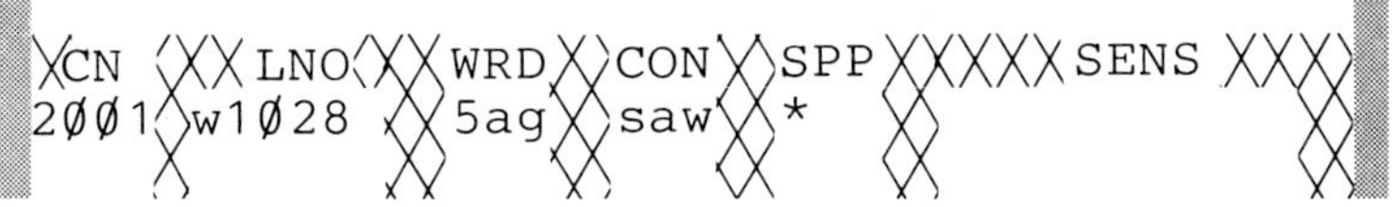

The organism isolated is a <u>Staphylococcus aureus</u>, and the three letter code for this is **SAU.** Type this in and it appears as a valid entry.

Hold down the open-apple key and press **DEL** [hold down the CTRL key and press X]. This moves the cursor to the left hand side of the SPP column and erases the sau entered. Now press ↓ [**CTRL+B**] then hold the **SHIFT** key down and press **A.** The shifted A character is the single letter code for Streptococcus group A which has a 3 letter code sga. The program has recognised the single character code, translated it into the 3 letter code on the screen and is now awaiting a susceptibility result with the cursor in the SENS column.

Press open-apple+DEL [CTRL+X] to delete this species code then press ↓ and then **S** which is the single character code for <u>St.aureus.</u>

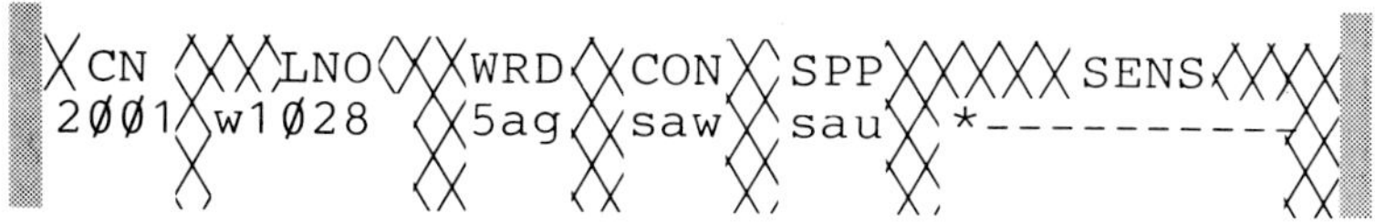

    Valid entries while the cursor is in this column are S, I, U, R and SPACE. These indicate sensitivity, intermediate sensitivity, sensitivity to urinary levels, resistance or not tested respectively. The space character appears on the screen as a horizontal bar. Try typing each of these. On the Apple IIe/IIc the program will also accept DEL, ⇐ and ⇒. The Apple II+ equivalents are ⇐, CTRL+A and ⇒. DEL and ⇐ move the cursor left one space, ⇒ moves the cursor right one space. Type in a sensitivity pattern and then use these controls. Note that it is impossible to move the cursor beyond the SENS column using these keys. Notice also that movement of the cursor using ⇐ [CTRL+A] and ⇒ does not affect the sensitivity pattern, although the cursor will obscure the underlying character. To move the cursor back to the SPP column one must press open-apple+DEL [CTRL+X], DEL [⇐] will not delete back from SENS to SPP. This is to prevent disastrous loss of entries from an accidental sustained keypress, which could otherwise delete all data entered at a session. Move the cursor to the left hand side of the SENS column and type in the following sensitivity pattern **SSSRSSSRSSS**. To complete the record entry press **RETURN**. The cursor moves to the next line on the left of the LNO column, ready for the next record

    With the cursor in this position the computer will accept any valid specimen type code, * for 'Help', ⌃ to record or DEL [⇐]. Press **DEL** [⇐]; the cursor moves back to the SENS column of the previous record to allow correction. Press open-apple+DEL [CTRL+X], then **DEL** [⇐] repeatedly to erase the record entered. Now try entering several records, using the delete facilities to correct any errors.

CN	LNO	WRD	CON	SPP	SENS
2001	w1028	5ag	cut	sau	sssrsssrsss
2002	u111	mog	wee	eco	suursi-----
2003	b128	icg	blo	eco	s--sssrssss
2004	f11956	mog	wee	sal	----------
2005	*				

To gain familiarity and confidence try deleting back through these records and re-entering a few. Any problems encountered should be resolved using the Reference Section of the manual. Then enter a full page of information.

CN	LNO	WRD	CON	SPP	SENS
2001	u392	gpg	???	eco	sssrsssssss-
2002	u411	dwg	???	kpn	rrrrusssssi-
2003	u413	uog	wee	pro	rrrrrssrss-
2004	u415	gog	gyn	cit	ussisssss-
2005	t417	6bg	bts	aci	rrrrrsrrrr-
2006	t419	6bg	fbc	pae	s-s--------
2007	t421	icp	blo	ent	rssrssssss-
2008	t423	icg	blo	ent	rrrrrrsrrr-
2009	t427	w3p	tot	pre	sssssssrss-
2010	s59	6ag	puo	mtu	sssssss----
2011	s62	w5p	tot	spn	sss--------
2012	s71	1ag	nut	spn	sss--------
2013	s72	isp	tot	mtu	rsssssss----
2014	s84	1ag	nut	hin	--ssss-----
2015	s91	1ag	rta	spn	sss--------
2016	s95	6ag	puo	mtu	sssssss----
2017	s96	jcb	???	spn	ssr--------
2018	s97	icp	gas	spn	sss--------
2019	s98	icp	gas	hin	--ssss-----
2020	*				

Now enter the next record **F27 RETURN AEP KID ROT RETURN.** When RETURN is pressed the screen clears and the entry table is redrawn with the last record at the top of the table and the cursor positioned at the start of the next entry. This is to allow deletion back for corrections, and to serve as a reminder of which record is to be entered next. Further entries can be made on the new table, up to a MAXIMUM OF 180 AT ANY ENTRY SESSION.

Review and Correction of Entries:-

The cursor is in the first position of the LNO column; press ^. The screen will clear and then display the entry table with a different header.

SENSITIVITY CHECK ROUTINE

Hit C to continue, W to correct

CN	LNO	WRD	CON	SPP	SENS
2001	u392	gpg	???	eco	sssrssssss-
2002	u411	dwg	???	kpn	rrrrussssi-
2003	u413	uog	wee	pro	rrrrrssrss-
2004	u415	gog	gyn	cit	ussissssss-
2005	t417	6bg	bts	aci	rrrrrsrrrr-
2006	t419	6bg	fbc	pae	s-s--------
2007	t421	icp	blo	ent	rssrssssss-
2008	t423	icg	blo	ent	rrrrrrsrrr-
2009	t427	w3p	tot	pre	sssssssrss-
2010	s59	6ag	puo	mtu	sssssss----
2011	s62	w5p	tot	spn	sss--------
2012	s71	1ag	nut	spn	sss--------
2013	s72	isp	tot	mtu	rssssss----
2014	s84	1ag	nut	hin	--ssss-----
2015	s91	1ag	rta	spn	sss--------
2016	s95	6ag	puo	mtu	sssssss----
2017	s96	jcb	???	spn	ssr--------
2018	s97	icp	gas	spn	sss--------
2019	s98	icp	gas	hin	--ssss-----
2020	f27	aep	kid	rot	-----------

This represents a chance to review entries made and correct them if necessary. Press **W**.

ENTRY CORRECTION ROUTINE

Which entry number? *
Press ^ to escape

Enter a number corresponding to that in the CN column for the entry which requires correction, for example **2Ø Ø1**, then press **RETURN.** (If this routine is accessed accidentally press ^ to return to the review table.)

The computer now checks to make sure that the computer reference number given corresponds to an entry made at this session. If it does not then an error message is returned and there is an opportunity to try again.

On input of a valid number the computer displays that entry at the top of a standard entry table, with the cursor over the specimen site position of the LNO column. The entry can be erased completely by pressing *, in which case the program erases the entry, reassigns serial computer numbers to the subsequent entries and reverts to the review routine. If the record requires correction then type the corrections over the incorrect entry displayed. In this case simply retype the isolate data; → can be used to skip over any columns which do not require correction. When the entry is complete press RETURN with the cursor in the SENS column. The computer will alter the entry and revert to the review routine.

So there is an opportunity to check that the entries are correct, and to alter or even erase incorrect records. When all the entries made at the current session have been reviewed on the screen (press **C** repeatedly) a message is displayed.

> Press R to record, C to review again

Press **C**; the current session entries are reviewed again. Press **R** and the information entered is recorded to disk.

Recording Entries to Disk:-

So press **R**. The screen clears and displays the message:-

> RECORDING DATA

The disk drive operates for a few minutes, according to how many new isolates have been entered. When the information has been successfully recorded on the PRIME DATA disk a message appears.

> O.K. Let's backup the data
>
> Place the backup disk in drive
>
>   Press any key to continue

Replace the prime data disk with the backup and press any key. Once more the computer will check to make sure that there is a disk in the drive and that it is the correct one. If not then the appropriate error correction is requested. Once the correct disk is in then the message:-

> Backing up data. This will take a while

will be displayed while the entries are recorded to the backup disk. When this is completed the screen clears and displays:-

> Your entries at this session have been added to the disk records as numbers:-
>   2001   to   2020
> inclusive
>
>   Press any key to continue

At this point it is advisable to enter in a logbook the date, first and last laboratory number recorded, first and last computer number (i.e. 2001, 2020) used and the week number. An example logbook for the dummy data is given in the Appendix. This is a useful record allowing the user to match a computer number interval to a time period over which the organisms were isolated. Press a key and you will be given an opportunity to return to the main Microbe Base menu. If you wish to continue with the exercises at this time press C, otherwise press E and the final message from the input program is displayed.

Take good care of the disks

The flashing cursor appears, indicating that the program has handed control back to the computer keyboard.

We hope that the session was not too arduous or frustrating. The level of computer familiarity among microbiologists seems to vary greatly and it is very difficult to write a manual suitable for the whole of this broad spectrum. We hope that you have developed some confidence in all the safety nets that have been incorporated in the program. We also hope that the messages on the screen are sufficiently lucid to guide the user through the programs with little reference to the manual.

RECOVERING INFORMATION

If you are continuing the exercises from the previous chapter, you should now see the Microbe Base main menu on your screen. Otherwise follow the startup instructions at the beginning of 'Information Entry' until this appears.

```
                        MICROBE BASE


Options Available:-

1) Enter susceptibility information

2) Recover information

3) Use summary routines

4) Use disk handling routines

5) Set up/alter description list

6) End program


Press a number (1-6)
```

The second exercise concerns the recovery of information. Press **2.** The screen displays the MICROBE BASE logo and the message 'PLEASE WAIT, LOADING RECOVERY PROGRAM', then displays the recall menu.

```
              SENSITIVITY RECALL ROUTINES


  Options available:-
  1) Obtain a summary
  2) Print results to printer
  3) Leaf through results
  4) Leaf through selected results
  5) Search for a result on a specimen
  6) Get operator instructions
  7) Get valid entry tables
  8) End program

 Press a number (1-8)
```

Each of these options is described below.

Option 3 - **Leaf through results routine**

Press **3** and the screen will display a message.

```
            LEAF THROUGH ROUTINE



     Place records disc in the drive
        Close the drive door

   Press any key to continue, E to end
```

Insert the PRIME DATA records disk and press **C**.

```
                LEAF  THROUGH  ROUTINE



    This is a prime disc
    with 2020 records on it
    entitled microbe base p

        Press any key to continue
```

The disc status, number of records and title are
displayed. Insertion of a disk which has not been
formated as a MICROBE BASE data disk results in an
error message and further instructions. Press **C**.

```
                LEAF  THROUGH  ROUTINE



    Enter lowest record number to retrieve
    (number from 1 to 2020)               *
```

A time interval for the search   is   being
requested. The computer numbers given to isolate
records have been recorded in a logbook in the
Appendix. Weeks 6-8 correspond to record numbers
1500-2000 so to search this interval type **1500,**
the lowest number of the interval. Nothing happens,
except that 1500 appears on the screen. This is
because the entry could be incomplete. To complete
the entry press **RETURN.**

```
                   LEAF THROUGH ROUTINE



        Enter lowest record number to retrieve
        (number from 1 to 2020)              1500

        Enter highest record number to retrieve
        (number from 1500 to 2020)              *
```

Type **2000** **RETURN**.

```
                   LEAF THROUGH ROUTINE

             Press C to continue, E to end

     cn      lno     wrd    con   spp         sens
    2000  u1345     gpg   ???   eco   sssssssssss-
    1999  u1342     gpg   ???   eco   sssssssssss-
    1998  u1340     gpg   ???   eco   sssssssssss-
    1997  b359      ssb   ???   pae   s-s---------
    1996  b358      ssb   ???   sga   sss---------
    1995  b357      ssb   ???   sga   sss---------
    1994  b355      w1p   tot   sau   rssssss-----
    1993  b352      w1p   tot   sau   rssssss-----
    1992  b350      8ag   obs   sau   rsssss------
    1991  y111      opg   see   spn   sss---------
    1990  y110      opg   see   spn   sss---------
    1989  s313      mog   puo   hin   --sssr------
    1988  s312      icp   gas   hin   --srsr------
    1987  s310      icg   blo   hin   --ssss------
    1986  s309      4ag   cap   hin   --ssss------
    1985  s306      4ag   cap   spn   sss---------
    1984  s304      4ag   sew   spn   sss---------
    1983  s302      3ag   hac   spn   sss---------
    1982  s300      3ag   cut   spn   sss---------
```

     There is a title line, showing which routine   is
being used, below which there are 1 or 2 operator
instruction lines, which give instructions   on   how
to move on to the next display. Below this   is   the

header line, which gives a title to each column of
information; cn is the computer's reference number
for the entry; the column lno contains the code for
type or site of specimen, and a laboratory
reference number; wrd indicates the ward or
department of origin; con indicates the consultant;
spp indicates the species and sens indicates the
antibiotic sensitivity of the organism.
   Note that the records are appearing in reverse
order of entry - i.e. the most recent first. Press
C to see more pages of results or E to end the
scan. Eventually a message is presented.

That's the lot
Press any key to continue

   Press any key to revert to the main recall menu.
Isolate records could be reviewed from a records
book without a computer, but would they be
presented neatly and legibly? Recall does have a
place in reviewing the information entered, and a
quick look at the past few weeks' work can give
some good clues as to the most profitable analyses
to try.

Option 4 - Leaf Through Selected Results

   From the main recall menu select option 4, 'Leaf
through selected results' by pressing **4.**

SELECTIVE LEAF THROUGH

Place records disc in the drive
Close the drive door

Press any key to continue, E to end

   Insert the BACKUP DATA records disk and press **C.**

```
                    SELECTIVE  LEAF  THROUGH



        This is a backup disc
        with 2Ø2Ø records on it
        entitled microbe base b

             Press any key to continue
```

    Notice that with this backup disc the computer
has given a different status (backup), and also a
different title. Press **C**.

```
                    SELECTIVE  LEAF  THROUGH



        Enter lowest record number to retrieve
        (number from 1 to 2Ø2Ø)              *
```

    To review the same record interval type **1511
RETURN**. This is an incorrect entry, but the display
is asking for the highest number for the search.

```
        Enter lowest record number to retrieve
        (number from 1 to 2Ø2Ø)            1511

        Enter highest record number to retrieve
        (number from 1511 to 2Ø2Ø)            *
```

    Press **DEL [←]**. The display clears and allows
re-entry of the low search number. Enter **15ØØ
RETURN 2ØØØ RETURN.** On completion of this
entry the selection menu is displayed.

<pre>
                  SELECTIVE LEAF THROUGH

     Hit S to select, D to deselect, I to
       ignore, B to block select or DEL to
                 return to a line
      1) Specimen type   *
      2) Ward
      3) Consultant
      4) Species
      5) Antibiotic 1
      6) Antibiotic 2
      7) Antibiotic 3
      8) Antibiotic 4
      9) Antibiotic 5
     10) Antibiotic 6
     11) Antibiotic 7
     12) Antibiotic 8
     13) Antibiotic 9
     14) Antibiotic 10
     15) Antibiotic 11
</pre>

To deal with the new concepts, the program requires a set of search criteria for selective review of the records. There are 15 portions, or 'fields' of the isolate record which these criteria refer to, specimen type, ward/department, consultant, species and each of the 11 sensitivity entries. The user is required to enter search criteria for each field. These criteria may be I, S, D or B. These are explained below. Do not enter any data when reading the next five paragraphs.

If I is specified then the field is ignored when the program examines records for selection.

If S is specified the program will then require a valid entry for the field. For instance if the user wishes to select blood culture specimens, and the cursor is opposite specimen type then press S to notify the computer that a specimen type is to be selected. The cursor moves across on the same

line after printing s and awaits a valid specimen
code. Press **B.** In this example the user has
specified that only records for isolates from blood
cultures will be considered for display. Now press
DEL [**<-**] to erase the entry and move the cursor
back to the search criteria column.

   If D is specified the program will then require
a valid entry for the field. For instance, if the
user wishes to select records which DO NOT
originate from mid stream urines, and the cursor is
opposite specimen type then press **D** to notify the
computer that a specimen type is to be deselected.
The cursor moves across on the same line after
printing d and awaits a valid specimen code.Press
U. In this example the user has specified that only
records for isolates which do not originate from
urines be considered for display. Press **DEL** [**<-**] to
erase the entry and move the cursor back to the
search criteria column.

   If B is specified the program will require two
valid entries for the field, for example, if the
user wishes to select records for the
Enterobacteriaceae group and the cursor was on the
same line as the 'Species' prompt, the user would
press B, then the code for the first of the species
in the Enterobacteriaceae block in the species
list, 'ECO', then the code for the last of the
Enterobacteriaceae in the block, 'SAL'. In this
example the user has specified that only records
with species codes in the block from eco to sal
inclusive in the species code list be considered
for display.

   B is not a valid search criterion for an
antibiotic field. I, S and D can be specified for
any field.

   The computer wants a set of search criteria;
resume typing in the keypresses designated in the
text. Search for mid stream urine specimens
containing E. coli from general practitioners as an
example. At the moment the cursor (*) is opposite
Specimen type. To select urines press **S.**

       1) Specimen type   s *
       2) Ward

Now specify the specimen type to select by pressing **U** for mid stream urines.

```
     1) Specimen type    s u
     2) Ward             *
```

To select for ward of origin press **S**.

```
     1) Specimen type    s u
     2) Ward             s *
```

Now type **1AG** - this is not a misprint, just an illustration of what to do when an error occurs.

```
     1) Specimen type    s u
     2) Ward             s 1ag
     3) Consultant       *
```

The last entry was incorrect, so press **DEL** [**<-**].

```
     1) Specimen type    s u
     2) Ward             *
     3) Consultant
```

Now correct the entry by typing **S**, then **GPG**.

```
     1) Specimen type    s u
     2) Ward             s gpg
     3) Consultant       *
```

The consultant field is to be ignored so press **I**.

```
     2) Ward             s gpg
     3) Consultant       i
     4) Species          *
```

To select for <u>E.coli</u> press **S**. As an illustration type **QQQ** which is not a valid species code. The program replies with an error beep and deletes the invalid entry. Press **DEL** [**<-**]. This gives an opportunity to alter the selection criterion. Press **S** and type **ECO** - the code for <u>E.coli</u> (alternatively press ↓ [CTRL+B] followed by e, the single character code for <u>E.coli</u>).

```
   3) Consultant        i
   4) Species           s eco
   5) Antibiotic 1       *
```

   Press **I** for each antibiotic and a message is displayed.

```
   15) Antibiotic 11      i

        Press any key to continue
```

Press any key.

SELECTIVE LEAF THROUGH

Options available:-

1) Print records to screen

2) Print records to printer

Press a number (1 or 2)

   This menu gives the choice of screen or printed copy of the selected results. Printed copy output is primarily designed for cases where evidence of a cross infection incident has been found and documentation is required for further discussions or to trace patient names on the basis of laboratory numbers. For the moment select screen print by pressing **1**.

```
              LEAF THROUGH ROUTINE

         Press C to continue, E to end

    cn      lno     wrd    con    spp         sens
    2000   u1345   gpg    ???   eco   sssssssssss-
    1999   u1342   gpg    ???   eco   sssssssssss-
    1998   u1340   gpg    ???   eco   sssssssssss-
    1947   u1307   gpg    ???   eco   sssssssssss-
    1946   u1306   gpg    ???   eco   sssssssssss-
    1945   u1300   gpg    ???   eco   sssssssssss-
    1944   u1285   gpg    ???   eco   sssssssssss-
    1943   u1280   gpg    ???   eco   sssssssssss-
    1942   u1279   gpg    ???   eco   sssssssssss-
    1865   u1196   gpg    ???   eco   sssssssssss-
    1864   u1189   gpg    ???   eco   sssssssssss-
    1841   u1129   gpg    ???   eco   sssssssssss-
    1840   u1127   gpg    ???   eco   sssssssssss-
    1829   u1124   gpg    ???   eco   sssssssssss-
    1828   u1121   gpg    ???   eco   sssssssssss-
    1827   u1119   gpg    ???   eco   sssssssssss-
    1826   u1117   gpg    ???   eco   sssssssssss-
    1825   u1115   gpg    ???   eco   sssssssssss-
    1753   u1021   gpg    ???   eco   sssssssssss-
```

Notice that it takes much longer to fill the screen this time, because many records had to be investigated before 19 fulfilling the criteria were found. This is another reason for use of the print option. The computer can be left sorting and printing whilst the user carries out other tasks. Notice also all the isolates are fully sensitive to all agents, but none have been tested against antibiotic 11 (Trial 2). Press C to delve further into the past, or, AT ANY TIME, press E to end the search and return to the main menu.

That was an example of a selective search. A few more to try at leisure, are:-

Flucloxacillin resistant <u>St.aureus</u> - Main menu, press 4, insert either disk, press C to continue, lowest record number 1, highest record number 400, I for site, I for ward, I for consultant, S SAU for species, I for antibiotic 1 (penicillin), S R for antibiotic 2 (flucloxacillin), and I for antibiotics 3-11 . These are rare, so the search will not produce many records.

Wound infections with <u>St.aureus</u> from surgical consultant CUT - Main menu, press 4, insert either disk, press C to continue, lowest record number 1, highest record number 600, S W for site, I for ward, S CUT for consultant, S SAU for species, and I for antibiotics 1-11.

Select screen or printer copy for these, but please remember IF YOU ARE ASKED TO CONNECT THE PRINTER MAKE SURE IT IS CONNECTED, SWITCHED ON AND HAS SUFFICIENT PAPER WHICH HAS BEEN CORRECTLY INSERTED before allowing the program to continue. It is not possible to incorporate a safety net here because of hardware design, so beware.

The selective recall routine is primarily designed to obtain the final proof on cross infection incidents on paper and to enable the laboratory to look up patient names for the isolates via the laboratory daybook, but can have many secondary uses.

Option 2 - Print Results to Printer
From the main menu press 2.

```
              PRINT RECORDS ROUTINE


        Place records disc in the drive
           Close the drive door

        Press any key to continue
```

Insert either records disk and press **C**.

```
              PRINT RECORDS ROUTINE




        This is a prime disk
        with 2020 records on it
        entitled microbe base p

             Press C to continue, E to end
```

Press **C,** then enter the lowest and highest record numbers to print, say 999 and 1017.

```
                 PRINT RECORDS ROUTINE


    Enter lowest record number to retrieve
    (number from 1 to 2Ø2Ø)          999

    Enter highest record number to retrieve
    (number from 999 to 2Ø2Ø)        1Ø17*
```

The screen clears and the user is asked to connect the printer:-

```
                 PRINT RECORDS ROUTINE



        Please connect the printer


        Press any key to continue
```

Ensure that the printer is connected, has sufficient paper which is correctly inserted and that it is switched on, then press any key. The printer will print the results in the following format:-

```
 999  nose swab   13   2ag wee E.coli            ssssssssss-
1000  catch urine  40   2ag wee E.coli            rrrrrssssrr-
1001  catch urine  42   1ag rta Aerob sporer      rrrrrsrrrs-
1002  catch urine  50   ang obs E.coli            ssssssssss-
1003  catch urine  53   sog ??? K.pneumoniae      rrrrssrrrs-
1004  catch urine  64   rog wee K.pneumoniae      rssssssssss-
1005  catch urine  70   rog wee Klebsielleae      sssrssssss-
1006  catch urine  71   mog puo E.coli            rrrrsssssss-
1007  catch urine  73   mog sbe E.coli            ssssssssss-
1008  catch urine  74   dwg ??? E.coli            ssssssssss-
1009  catch urine  80   aeg ??? E.coli            rssssssssss-
1010  catch urine  90   gog gyn P.mirabilis       sssssssrsr-
1011  catch urine  91   bog ??? E.coli            ssssssssss-
1012  blood cultur 10   4ag hip St.aureus         rsssss-----
1013  blood cultur 15   5bg saw St.aureus         rsssss-----
1014  pus           2   1ag nut St.aureus         ssssss-----
1015  pus           4   gpg ??? St.aureus         rsssss-----
1016  pus           9   aeg ??? St.aureus         ssssss-----
1017  ear swab      1   aeg ??? St.aureus         ssssss-----
```

The computer reference number for the entry is
on the left; the next column contains the type or
site of specimen, a laboratory reference number,
the ward or department code, the consultant code,
the species name and the antibiotic sensitivity of
the organism.

Whilst the printer is operating a message is
displayed.

```
        PRINT RECORDS ROUTINE



              Printing

          Press E to stop
```

Press E to abort the print run and return to the
main menu if neccesary. Eventually a message will
be displayed.

```
            That's the lot
        Press any key to continue
```

Press any key to revert to the main recall menu.

The main purpose of this routine is to provide printed copy of results for a paper record system, or to read at leisure.

Option 1 - Summary

This is the most powerful and flexible analysis facility. It can be accessed from both the loader program main menu and the recovery program main menu. Press **1** in the recovery main menu. The computer will ask for the PROGRAMS disk.

```
                SUMMARY ROUTINE



      Place programs disk in the drive
            Close the drive door


        Press any key to continue
```

Insert the correct disk and press **C**.

```
                SUMMARY ROUTINE


                LOADING ROUTINE
```

The drive will operate and a selection menu will appear.

```
                   SUMMARY ROUTINE

        Hit S to select, D to deselect, B to
        block select, C to count, I to ignore
              or DEL to erase an error

         1) Specimen type        *
         2) Ward
         3) Consultant
         4) Species
         5) Antibiotic 1
         6) Antibiotic 2
         7) Antibiotic 3
         8) Antibiotic 4
         9) Antibiotic 5
        10) Antibiotic 6
        11) Antibiotic 7
        12) Antibiotic 8
        13) Antibiotic 9
        14) Antibiotic 10
        15) Antibiotic 11
```

This is similar to the selective leaf through selection menu and operates in the same fashion. There is an additional selection option C for count. Suppose that there is a query on blood cultures containing St.aureus from the past 500 records. The user wishes to know which wards were involved, how many isolates originated from each ward, and requires a susceptibility breakdown. To select for specimen type, press **S** then **B** indicating selection for site code b, i.e. blood culture isolates. To obtain details of the wards involved press **C** for count.

```
         1) Specimen site        s   b
         2) Ward                  c
         3) Consultant            *
         4) Species
```

The consultant field is not relevant to this search, either in terms of selecting records, or returning figures of isolate frequency by

consultant. Press **I** to ignore this field. Press **S**
and then **SAU** to select isolates of <u>St.aureus</u> only.

```
1) Specimen site      s b
2) Ward               c
3) Consultant         i
4) Species            s sau
5) Antibiotic 1       *
```

A complete analysis of the sensitivity patterns
of these isolates is required so press **C** for each
antibiotic, then **C** to continue.
The program checks that the search criteria will
produce a printout of results. If the criteria C, D
or B are used for any of the fields the program
will produce a printout for selected isolate
records, if only I and S are used throughout the
program will return to a blank search criteria menu
and await criteria which will give a printout. The
search criteria entered will produce a printout as
the fields Ward and Antibiotics 1-11 are to be
counted, so the program asks for the printer to be
connected.

```
          SUMMARY ROUTINE


      Please connect the printer

      Press any key when ready
```

Ensure that the printer is connected, switched
on and has adequate paper which is correctly
inserted, then press **C.** The printer gives a hard
copy of the selection criteria.

Selection criteria:-

Specimen type	Select	blood culture
Ward	Count	
Consultant	Ignore	
Species	Select	S.aureus
Antibiotic 1	Count	
Antibiotic 2	Count	
Antibiotic 3	Count	
Antibiotic 4	Count	
Antibiotic 5	Count	
Antibiotic 6	Count	
Antibiotic 7	Count	
Antibiotic 8	Count	
Antibiotic 9	Count	
Antibiotic 10	Count	
Antibiotic 11	Count	

The program requests that the programs disk be inserted, and that the user press **C** when ready. On completion of this the secondary analysis program is loaded.

```
                   SUMMARY ROUTINE


                   Loading routine
```

The program then asks for a data disk.

```
                   SUMMARY ROUTINE


         Place records disk in the drive
                Close the drive door

            Press any key to continue
```

Insert the prime data disk and press any key.

```
                    SUMMARY ROUTINE


This is a Prime disk
entitled microbe base p
With 2Ø2Ø records on

Press C if you wish to search this disk,
E if not
```

Press **C.** The program will then request specification of the search interval.

```
                    SUMMARY ROUTINE


Enter lowest record number to retrieve
(number from 1 to 2Ø2Ø)        *
```

This routine is identical to those used in the leaf through and search routines of the recovery program. Enter a low number **15ØØ** and a high number **2ØØØ.** The program requests that the printer be connected, and when this is done prints a hard copy of the disk details and search interval.

```
Disk title      = microbe base p
Disk status     = Prime
Lowest number   = 1500
Highest number  = 2000
```

The disk search commences.

```
                    SUMMARY ROUTINE



    Go away and be quiet. Searching


    Press E to end program in emergency
```

    Find something else to do for about 2 minutes to allow the computer to search through the 500 records.
    When the search of the disk is complete the screen will show:-

SUMMARY ROUTINE

Do you wish to extend this search to
another disk? (Y/N)

    This option allows the search to be extended over several disks if required, an overall summation being printed in hard copy. Press **N.** Follow the instructions displayed. The printer will print out the results of the search. Note that if one of the possible valid entries of a counted field has a count of zero that entry will not be listed, this is called null result suppression. As an example no blood culture isolates of <u>St.aureus</u> have occured on the coronary care unit, hence this unit does not appear in the printout of counts by ward. It is possible that a short search interval of very stringent search criteria will result in no isolate record fulfilling the search criteria being found. In this case only the field headings will be printed, and the printout for the number of records satisfying the criteria will be zero.

Wards:-

4ag	2
4bg	4
8ag	1
icg	2
ccg	1
rtg	1
w1p	2
w4p	1
w5p	1
icp	3
ssb	1

St. aureus

Antibiotic	Tested	NoTest	Sens	Inter	Urine	Resis	%Sen	%Int	%Uri	%Res
Penicillin	19	0	3	0	0	16	16	0	0	84
Fluclox	19	0	16	0	0	3	84	0	0	16
Fusidic acid	19	0	18	0	0	1	95	0	0	5
Gentamicin	19	0	16	0	0	3	84	0	0	16
Chloramphen	19	0	19	0	0	0	100	0	0	0
Tetracycline	19	0	16	0	0	3	84	0	0	16
Vancomycin	0	19	0	0	0	0				
Clindamycin	0	19	0	0	0	0				
Erythromycin	0	19	0	0	0	0				
Trial 1	0	19	0	0	0	0				
Trial 2	0	19	0	0	0	0				

Total records searched   - 501

Records satisfying criteria- 19

The printed data shows the number of isolates fulfilling the search criteria for each ward, ie there were 4 <u>St.aureus</u> isolated from blood cultures from ward 4A at the General Hospital during the search period. Of 19 <u>St.aureus</u> isolates from blood cultures 3 were sensitive to penicillin and 16 resistant, giving 16% sensitive and 84% resistant. All 19 were not tested for susceptibility to clindamycin.

On completion of printing the program provides 3 options, to print another summary, to return to the main Microbe Base menu, or to end the program. Select option 2 or 3 according to whether you wish to continue to further exercises in this session or not.

Other suggestions for summary searches are:-

1) Total printout of data on blood cultures. From the summary selection menu press **S B** to select blood culture isolates, then **C** for every other field. Search records 1 to 2000 on either data disk. This search takes about 10 minutes and gives a printout of numbers of positive blood cultures from each ward, each consultant, number of isolates for each species and a susceptibility summary.

2) Susceptibility of <u>St.aureus</u> isolated from in-patients at the General Hospital. From the summary selection menu press **I** for specimen type, **B** 1AG RTG to block select all wards at the General Hospital, **I** for consultant, **S SAU** for species, and **C** for each antibiotic field. Search records 1 to 2000 on either data disk.

3) Distribution of <u>Serratia</u> <u>spp</u>. From the summary selection menu press **I** for specimen type, **C** for ward, **I** for consultant, **S SER** for species and **I** for each antibiotic. Search records 1 to 200 on either disk. This search gives the frequency of isolation of <u>Serratia</u> for each ward.

Option 6 - Operator Instructions

From the main Microbe Base menu select the appropriate option to reload the information

recovery routines. From the main recovery menu
press **6.**

Place programs disk in drive
Close the drive door

Press any key to continue

Insert the disk and press **C.** The first page of
user instructions is displayed.

When the computer is turned off, start
Microbe Base as follows: insert the
PROGRAMS disk into Drive 1, close
the drive door, and switch the computer
on. Microbe Base will then start
automatically. If the power is
already on, you can start or restart
the program by inserting the PROGRAMS
disk and pressing the Open-Apple, CTRL
and RESET keys simultaneously. The
computer will request a valid 3-letter
operator code before allowing access to
the routines.

In all routines, the user will be
informed of errors by a beep, sometimes
accompanied by an error message. A
beep does not always mean an error; it
is sometimes used just to alert the
user to an unusual condition.

Press C to continue or E to end

This is the same as the operator instruction
option accessed in the information entry exercise.
Press C for each new page or E to return to the
main recovery menu.

Option 7 - Valid Entry Tables

This is the same 'Help' facility for valid codes as accessed in the information entry exercise.
From the main recovery menu press **7**.

SENSITIVITY RECALL ROUTINES

Would you like to see the valid entry
list for:-

1) Specimen type
2) Wards
3) Consultants
4) Species
5) Return to main menu

Press the appropriate number (1-5)

This allows access to the information in the description file - i.e. the entries which the computer has been told to recognise as acceptable.
Press **1** to review the acceptable specimen site codes, then **C** to revert to the menu. Press **2** to review the valid ward entries, then **C** to return to the main menu. Press **3** to review valid consultant codes, then **C** to return to the main menu. Press **4** to review valid species codes. Press **C** to review the species data pages or **E** to end the review. Press **C** then **5** to return to the main menu.

Option 5 - Search for a Result on a Specimen

From the recovery menu press **5**.

```
          SEARCH FOR A SPECIMEN BY NUMBER



       Place records disk in the drive
           Close the drive door

         Press any key to continue
```

Insert the prime data disk and press **C.**

```
        SEARCH FOR A SPECIMEN BY NUMBER



     This is a prime disk
     with 2Ø2Ø records on it
     entitled microbe base p

           Press any key to continue
```

Press **C.** Now enter the lowest and highest numbers for the search, **457 RETURN** and **511.**

```
        SEARCH FOR A SPECIMEN BY NUMBER



     Enter lowest record number to retrieve
     (number from 1 to 2Ø2Ø)        457

      Enter highest record number to retrieve
     (number from 457 to 2Ø2Ø)        511
```

Press **RETURN** to complete the entry.

```
        SEARCH FOR A SPECIMEN BY NUMBER

     Enter specimen type and number   *
```

A valid specimen type code and a number of 1 to 5 digits is required. Type **W 2 5 Ø RETURN.** The screen displays the data review table and searches for any entries with the specimen code w and the laboratory number 250 in the specified range.

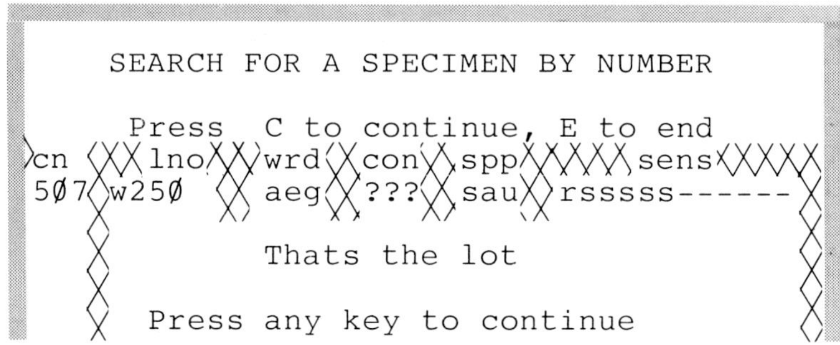

Press **C** and the display reverts to the recovery menu.

MICROBE BASE was designed with the philosophy that recovery of information by patient name or specimen   number   is   fairly   easy   in   most laboratories. The main purpose of the programs is to enable the user to sort the information by other,   more   complex   criteria,   nonetheless this routine does give some capability to retrieve by laboratory number.

Option 8 - End program

To exit from the data recovery routines, end the current routine and select option **8** from the menu. The program then allows you to return to the main Microbe Base menu by pressing C or to end the session by pressing E.

DISK HANDLING ROUTINES

GETTING STARTED:-

These routines enable the user to format new data or description file disks, copy or archive data disks, alter the status of a data disk or alter the apparent number of entries on a data disk. In this section the use of these routines and the method for altering an incorrect record which has been recorded to disk will be illustrated. In addition disks will be formatted which the user will require to set up his own records system. **Three new unformatted disks are required to complete these exercises** (see Precautions and Advice).

From the main Microbe Base menu select option **4**. The MICROBE BASE logo will appear together with the message 'PLEASE WAIT LOADING DISK HANDLER', followed by the disk handling menu.

```
                    DISK HANDLING


    Options available:-

    1) Alter current disk status
    2) Alter current max record number
    3) Format a new records disk
    4) Format a new description list disk
    5) Archive 1200 records
    6) Copy a data disk
    7) End program


    Press a number (1-7)
```

Option 1 - Alter Disk Status

   This option can be used to alter a backup disk
to a prime or to protect a pair of data disks from
further entry by altering their status to Archive.
To keep past data on the MICROBE BASE system simply
fill each pair of records disks, alter the status
of both to Archive, and store them for future
reference, starting further records on a fresh
Prime/Backup pair.
   Select option **1** from the menu.

```
                  ALTER DISK STATUS



              Please insert the disk

              Press C to continue
```

Insert the PRIME data disk and press **C**.

```
                  ALTER DISK STATUS


       This is a prime data disk
       with 2020 records on it
       entitled microbe base p

                  Press C to continue
```

Press **C**.

```
       Would you like the status to be Prime,
               Backup or Archive

               (Press P, B or A)
```

   Press **A** to make this an archive disk. The drive
will run for a few seconds and then the program
will revert to the disk handling menu.
   To prove that the status has been altered select
option **1** again and reinsert the disk. Press **C** again

and note that the disk status is now Archive. Now
press **C** and reset the status to prime by pressing
P, so that others will be able to carry out these
exercises.

Option 2 - Alter Current Maximum Record Number

   The main uses of this option are to erase a
batch of erroneous results and to alter a bad
record which has already been recorded to disk.
Select option **2 from the menu, insert the PRIME**
data disk and press
C.

```
            ALTER CURRENT MAX RECORD NUMBER


   This is a prime data disk
   with 2Ø2Ø records on it
   entitled microbe base p

            Press C to continue
```

Press **C.**

```
   Enter the new maximum number
   (Enter a number from Ø to 96ØØ   then

                press RETURN

                     *
```


   The program will accept numeric keypresses and
DEL only. It will not accept a number outside the
range specified. Enter the new maximum record
number **2ØØØ.** Then press **RETURN.** This will
restore the number of accessible records to 2000
again for others who may use the disk for the
exercises. The program will alter the number and
return to the disk handling menu. Alter the number
of records on the backup disk in the same way.

   To alter a record on disk, first find the

computer number of the record, and the total number of records on the disk using the data recovery routines. Then alter the current disk number on BOTH THE PRIME AND BACKUP DISKS to one less than the number of the record to be altered. Use the data entry routines to enter the record correctly, reload the disk handling routines and alter the maximum record number back to its original value on both PRIME and BACKUP disks. This is an arduous process, but the operator has several opportunities to detect errors in data input and should be encouraged to correct errors at an early stage.

Option 3 – Format a New Records Disk

This routine is used to format new data disks. They are checked for faults and then formatted as Archive data disks. Their status may be altered by use of option 1 subsequently. Only new unformatted disks can be formatted.

Take two new disks and write labels for each, calling one Prime 1 and the other Backup 1. Label the first, select option **3** from the disk handling menu.

```
                FORMAT A NEW DATA DISK


   NOTE WELL THE DISK WILL BE COMPLETELY
                  OVERWRITTEN
   I suggest that you remove the disk from
   the drive and check that you wish to
   reformat it, then press E to return to
   menu or C to continue
```

Insert the disk and press **C**.

```
                FORMAT A NEW DATA DISK



        Enter the disk title of up to 16
        letters, then press RETURN
                     *
```

Enter the title for your first prime data disk.
It should indicate the status of the disk, the
description file it will be used with and the date
when it is first used, for example 'routine p
aug85'. Then press **RETURN**.

```

                FORMAT A NEW DATA DISK


    I am about to overwrite this disk
    and title it xxxxxxxxxxxxxxxx
    Hit C to continue or E to revert to menu

```

    This is the final opportunity to remove the disk
if it has programs or data on it. Press **C.** The
drive will operate for 1 minute.

```

                FORMAT A NEW DATA DISK


    The disk  is  reformatted  as  a  data  disk

                  Press C to continue

```

    Press **C** and the program reverts to the disk
handling menu. Process the second disk in the same
way, then use option 1 to alter their status to
Prime and Backup as appropriate. These are the
disks which will be used to enter data on your own
system.

Option 4 – **Format a Description List Disk**

    This routine is used to format a disk on which
to store copies of description files and password
files. The user may wish to operate more than one
database system using the programs disk,   for
example a general routine susceptibility data on
one data disk set and a patient oriented Special
Care Baby Unit version on another set. Also the
description file may be altered from time to time,
and the user will wish to retain copies of the old

versions so that valid searches of records written
under them can be carried out. These files can be
retained on   a   description file disk,   and
transferred to the programs disk for use as will be
described in the next chapter.

   Take a new unformatted disk and label   it
'Description files'. Select option **4** from the disk
handling menu. The program will request a disk.
Insert the disk and press **C**.

          FORMAT A NEW DESCRIPTION LIST DISK

  NOTE WELL THE DISK WILL BE COMPLETELY
                  OVERWRITTEN
  I suggest that you remove the disk from
  the drive and check that you wish to
  reformat it, then press E to return to
  menu or C to continue

Press **C.**

          FORMAT A NEW DESCRIPTION LIST DISK

              Enter the disk title
               then press RETURN
               *

   Enter the title of the description file disk,
for example 'desc files 85-'. The program will
accept an entry of characters, letters, spaces or
numbers, and DEL. Press **RETURN** to complete the
entry.

```
        FORMAT A NEW DESCRIPTION LIST DISK


   I am about to overwrite this disk
   and title it xxxxxxxxxxxxxxx
   Hit C to continue or E to revert to menu
```

This is the final opportunity to remove the disk if it has programs or data on it. Press **C**. The drive will operate for one minute.

```
        FORMAT A NEW DESCRIPTION LIST DISK


   The disk is reformatted as a data disk

            Press C to continue
```

Press **C** and the program reverts to the disk handling menu. Remove the disk and store it for use in the description file writer exercises.

Option 5 - Archive 1200 Records

This routine is used in conjunction with a 'rolling records' system. There are two approaches to storing old data. When a pair of current records disks (backup and prime) are full (9600 records) they can simply be altered to archive status, stored and a new pair of current records disks generated via disk handling. This is the simplest approach. Alternatively the number of records on the current disks can be maintained at 8000-9500 by regular archiving of data to an archive disk using this routine. DO NOT ATTEMPT TO ARCHIVE FROM THE DUMMY DATA DISKS. If you wish to carry out this out as a practical exercise do so on a copy of the dummy data disks generated via option 6 of the disk handling menu.
Select option **5** from the disk handling menu.

```
                    ARCHIVE DISK ROUTINE


            Please insert the program disk

               Press C to continue
```

Insert the program disk and press **C**.

```
                    ARCHIVE DISK ROUTINE


     Does you have one disk drive or two?(1/2)
```

Answer by pressing **1 RETURN** if you have a single
drive or **2 RETURN** if you have two. The program
requests a disk.

```
                    ARCHIVE DISK ROUTINE


      Please insert the disk to archive from
    This   disk   must   have   more    than
   12ØØ
    records
                Press C to continue
```

Insert the sender disk, ie the disk which has
the data to be copied. This MUST have more than
1200 accessible records, or it will be rejected
with an error message. Press **C**.

```
    This is a xxxxx disk
    with xxxx records
    entitled xxxxxxxxxxxxxxxx
    Do you wish to archive from this disk?
```

Press **Y**.

```
                ARCHIVE DISK ROUTINE


    Please insert the disk to copy to
 This disk must have less than 84Ø1
 records

             Press C to continue
```

Press **C**. The program is asking for a receiver disk on which to copy the records 1-1200 from the sender disk. Insert the archive disk. This MUST be a data disk with archive status, and space for a further 1200 records. Insert the receiver disk and press **C**.

```
 This is a xxxxx disk
 with xxxx records
 entitled xxxxxxxxxxxxxxxx
 Do you wish to archive to this disk?
```

Press **Y**. The computer marks the sender and receiver disks as such and will not accept an incorrect disk for processing.

```
                ARCHIVE DISK ROUTINE


    Please insert the disk to archive from
             Press C to continue
```

Insert the sender disk and press **C**. The drive will operate for about 4 minutes, and then request the receiver disk. Insert this and press **C**. The message changes to 'Archiving to this disk', and the drive runs for 4 minutes, then asks for the sender disk. Insert the sender disk and press **C**. The drive will operate for 5 minutes and then display the message 'The disk has been archived', 'Press C to continue'. Press **C** and the screen reverts to the disk handling menu. The records on the sender disk will be moved down to make room for a further 1200 records on the disk. THE COMPUTER NUMBER OF EACH RECORD RETAINED ON THE DISK WILL BE LOWERED BY 1200. This should be noted in the

database log sheet. Note that BOTH the prime and backup disks should be archived at the same session.
   The routine as described applies to single drive systems, the dual drive systems perform the same task but use both drive slots and are more rapid, simply follow the screen instructions for the dual drive versions.

Option 6 - Copy a Data Disk

This routine allows the user to make a copy of a data disk. The receiver disk must be formatted as a data disk prior to use in this routine. All the data on the sender disk up to and including the last accessable record number will be copied to the receiver disk. ANY PREVIOUSLY RECORDED DATA ON THE RECEIVER DISK WILL BE ERASED. This section is not intended as a practical exercise.
   Select option **6** from the disk handling menu.

```
                  COPY DISK ROUTINE


        Please insert the program disk

          Press C to continue
```

Insert the program disk and press **C**.

```
                COPY DISK ROUTINE


   Does you one disk drive or two? (1/2)
```

   Answer by pressing **1 RETURN** if you have a single drive or **2 RETURN** if you have a dual drive. The program requests a disk.

```
                    DISK COPY


     Please insert the disk to copy from
            Press C to continue
```

Insert the sender disk and press **C**.

```
This is a xxxxx disk
with xxxx records
entitled xxxxxxxxxxxxxxxx
Do you wish to copy from this disk?(y/n)
```

Press **Y**.

```
                    DISK COPY


     Please insert the disk to copy to
      NOTE THIS DISK WILL BE OVERWRITTEN
            Press C to continue
```

Insert a disk which has been formatted as a data
disk and press **C**.

```
This is an archive disk
with 0 records
entitled xxxxxxxxxxxxxxx
Do you wish to copy onto this disk?(y/n)
```

Press **Y**.

```
                    DISK COPY


     Please insert the disk which you are
                copying from
            Press C to continue
```

The sender and receiver disks are marked as
such. Reinsert the sender disk and press **C**. The
drive will operate for about 4 minutes, copying the

first 1200 records from the disk into memory. Then
the program asks for the receiver disk, insert this
and press **C**. The drive operates as the records are
written to the disk. This cycle is repeated until
all the data on the sender has been copied. Finally
a message appears.

DISK COPY

The disk has been copied
Press C to continue

The sender disk has now been copied to the
receiver disk. Press **C**, the program returns to the
disk handling menu.
  The routine as described applies to single drive
systems, the dual drive systems perform the same
task but use both drive slots and are more rapid,
simply follow the screen instructions for the dual
drive versions.

DESCRIPTION FILE WRITER

The routines accessed under the title 'Description file writer' enable the user to modify the lists of recognised codes for specimen type, ward, consultant and species, collectively referred to as the description list or description file and to manipulate these files on disk. They enable the programs to be tailored to a particular laboratory or use. Routines are also provided which allow the user to modify the list of valid passwords.

From the main Microbe Base menu select option 5 'Set up/alter description list'. The MICROBE BASE logo appears along with the message 'PLEASE WAIT, LOADING LIST WRITER'.

DESCRIPTION FILE WRITER

This program allows you to write a file consisting of details of the specimen type, ward and consultant codes which you wish to use, along with 3 and 1 letter codes for bacterial species, species names, names of the antibiotics tested and a list of all antibiotic names used. You can also use this program to alter or review the password list.
There are limits on numbers involved.
A maximum of 100 species, 100 antibiotic names, 120 wards, 120 consultants, 50 specimen types and 100 passwords can be specified. Think carefully about what you are going to do; altering a description file is a time consuming task.

Press any key to begin.

Press **C.** A menu appears.

```
                DESCRIPTION FILE WRITER

    What would you like to do:-

    1) Alter/review specimen codes

    2) Alter/review ward codes

    3) Alter/review consultant codes

    4) Alter/review antibiotic names

    5) Alter/review species name etc

    6) Record description file to disk

    7) Alter/review password file

    8) Record password file to disk

    9) End program

    Hit a number (1-9)
```

Press **1.** Since no data file has been loaded the
following screen is displayed.

```
                DESCRIPTION FILE WRITER

    Please insert the disk which contains
    the description file you are working on

         Press C to continue, E to escape
```

Press **C.** The drive operates and the program asks
for the description file name.

DESCRIPTION FILE WRITER

Type in the file name then hit return

(Use DEL to correct an error)

$

Press keys **S E N S SPACE D A T A** then **RETURN.** If the correct disk is in the drive and the file title has been entered correctly the screen displays the message "Loading data", otherwise an appropriate error message is displayed. When the data is loaded, you will see a list of valid specimen data displayed on the screen. For now press **C** to escape then **N** when asked if you want a printout. This will return you to the main description menu.

Now select option **6**; the message 'Record file as "SENS DATA"?' will appear. Press **N** and you will be prompted for a new file name.

DESCRIPTION FILE WRITER

Type in the file name then hit RETURN

(Use DEL to correct an error)

$

Press keys **D E M O SPACE D A T A** then **RETURN.** You will be asked to insert the disk to write to. Remove the programs disk from the drive and replace it with the description file disk which you formatted using the disk handling routines in the last chapter. (If you do not have this disk then press **E**, select option 9 of the list writer menu, remove the disk and press **E** which terminates the program.)

DESCRIPTION LIST WRITER

Recording description file demo data

The drive will operate for about 30 seconds, and then ask the operator to press any key to continue. Press **C.** The display reverts to the description file writer main menu. The demonstration description file has now been preserved for others to use in working through the earlier chapters.

To preserve the password code file for the demonstration data select option **7.** Insert the programs disk and press **C** to continue. Press the keys **C O D E S RETURN** when the file title is requested.

```
              DESCRIPTION LIST WRITER

Current passwords are:-

   No Code No Code No Code No Code No Code
    0  jtm  1        2        3        4
    5       6        7        8        9
   10      11       12       13       14
   15      16       17       18       19




Would you like to alter a code or go on
              Press A or G
```

Press **G.** The message 'Would you like a printout of these codes', 'Type Y or N' appears. Press **N** to return to the menu, then select option **8** 'Record password file to disk', insert the description file disk and record the password file, typing **D E M O** SPACE **C O D E S RETURN** when a file title is requested.

Once these files have been preserved the data can be modified as required for a new system. To elucidate a few points, the programs look for a description file called 'sens data' and a password file called 'codes' on the programs disk, and use the information which they find there as the valid input lists. The description file writer program can take a description file and password file from a description file disk and replace (overwrite) 'sens data' and 'codes'. This means that the demonstration valid data lists can be replaced by a new tailor made set. These routines will in fact allow several description lists to be preserved under different titles on the description list disk. These can be exchanged to the programs disk at will, allowing several versions of the program to be operated concurrently.

Another point to note is that the computer actually records a list number rather than a code for each field of an entry. For example, if a record is entered as originating from ward 1ag the computer finds that 1ag is valid entry 33 in the ward list and so records the ward as 33. On recall the ward code which is 33rd in the list is printed as being the ward of origin. The user can alter the codes via the list writer routines and if he has altered ward 33 to 20g then the program will display 20g as the ward rather than 1ag in the recover data programs. THE CONSEQUENCES OF ALTERING A DESCRIPTION LIST WHICH IS IN CURRENT USE SHOULD BE CAREFULLY ASSESSED. This effect can be useful, for example, if consultant 'saw' left and was replaced by 'new' who treated the same group of patients then the code could altered to 'new' via list writer and the date of the change noted in the program log sheet. New wards, specimen types, consultants, species and antibiotics can be added to the end of the list. It is recommended that careful records are kept of alterations to description files, noting the change made and the record number intervals and disk titles for which the old file is valid. An example is given in the log sheet in the Appendix. The old description file should be preserved on the description file disk in case the file is required to scan the data written using it.

The options which record a description file to disk, read a password file, and record a password file have been reviewed above. The remaining options allow the user to alter the codes and other information in the data lists of a description file. NOTE WELL the alterations made do not become incorporated into the description file until it is recorded to disk. If the user attempts to record a file under a title which is already in use on the disk a warning is printed, and the user is given the option of returning to the main menu to try again or to overwrite the old file. AN OLD FILE WHICH HAS BEEN OVERWRITTEN CANNOT BE RECOVERED, hence it is good practice to keep a backup copy of each file.

Option 1 – Review/alter specimen codes

From the description file writer main menu press 1.

```
               DESCRIPTION FILE WRITER

Current specimen codes are:-
No Code      Name        No Code      Name
 Ø ?     not known        1 u     catch urine
 2 t     csu              3 w     wound swab
 4 b     blood cultur     5 s     sputum
 6 g     genital swab     7 c     csf
 8 f     faeces           9 m     pm tissue
1Ø p     pus             11 a     aspirate
12 d     capd fluid      13 v     valve/shunt
14 e     ear swab        15 y     eye swab
16 n     nose swab       17 h     throat swab
18 x     enviromental    19 z     tissue
2Ø                       21
22                       23
24

Press C to escape, A to alter an entry
or G to go on
```

Press **A.** The message at the bottom of the screen becomes:-

> Press C to escape, or enter the number
>   of the entry which is to be altered
> ie Ø to 2Ø then hit RETURN
>   *

The program is waiting for the list number of the entry to be altered. Press **8,** then RETURN. The message changes.

> Alter 1-character code? (Y/N)

Press **Y** to alter the code.

> Enter new 1-character code: *.

Type in B.

> Sorry I can't accept that. Your entry
> B is identical to code 4

The computer will not accept a code which already appears in the list. The ONLY exception is ? (??? in the case of three letter codes), which can appear several times. Press any key; you will again be prompted for a 1 character code.

Press **J.** The new code is accepted, and the message 'Alter name? (Y/N)' appears. Press **N.** The screen is redrawn, with the single letter code for 8 as j.

To erase a code press **A, 19 RETURN,** and then **Y.** The screen is redrawn with no code or name for 19. ONLY the last filled entry in any list can be erased.

Now alter the codes back to the original form. Press **A, 8 RETURN, Y** in answer to the prompts, and then enter the original code **F.** Next press **Y** in response to 'Alter name? (Y/N)'.

> Enter new name (15 characters maximum)
> Then hit RETURN
> $

Type in **T I S S U E RETURN.** The screen is

redrawn with this name opposite 19. Now type **G**.

> Would you like a printout of these
>
> codes. Type Y or N

Press **Y**.

> Please connect the printer, switch it
> on and press any key

Connect the printer and press **C**. The printer produces a printout of the codes and names and returns to the Description File Writer menu.

Option 2 – **Alter/Review Ward Codes**

From the Description File Writer Main menu press **2**.

```
                 DESCRIPTION FILE WRITER

Current ward codes are:-
 No Code No Code No Code No Code No Code
  Ø   ???  1   ??g  2   1ag  3  1bg   4  2ag
  5   2bg  6   3ag  7   3bg  8  4ag   9  4bg
 1Ø   5ag 11   5bg 12   6ag 13  6bg  14  7ag
 15   7bg 16   8ag 17   8bg 18  9ag  19  icg
 2Ø   ccg 21   rtg 22   thg 23  occ  24  ??p
 25   w1p 26   w2p 27   w3p 28  w4p  29  w5p
 3Ø   w6p 31   icp 32   isp 33  thp  34  ??b
 35   jsb 36   jtb 37   ssb 38  jcb  39  thb
 4Ø   ?og 41   aeg 42   sog 43  org  44  mog
 45   gpg 46   dwg 47   eng 48  ang  49  uog
 5Ø   hag 51   pag 52   gog 53  dug  54  deg
 55   opg 56   bog 57   rog 58  gud  59  ?op

Press C to escape, A to alter an entry
or G to go on
```

The procedure for alteration and deletion of entries is similar to that for specimen codes, except that the option to alter code name no longer applies and three letter, rather than 1 letter codes are entered. Note that 59 is not the last filled entry, and so cannot be erased. The last entry is number 68, pap, which is on the second page of ward codes, accessed by pressing **G** in reply to the prompt.

Option 3 - Alter/Review Consultant Codes

From the Description File Writer Menu press **3**.

```
                DESCRIPTION FILE WRITER

Current consultant codes are:-
     Ø   ???   1   cut   2   sew   3 hac     4 dia
     5   puo   6   sbe   7   nut   8 rta     9 wee
    1Ø   uti  11   nsu  12   pid  13 obs    14 see
    15   saw  16   hip  17   cap  18 kid    19 tot
    2Ø   nip  21   bts  22   fbc  23 gas    24 blo
    25   doa  26   ded  27   gyn  28 tab    29
    3Ø        31        32        33        34
    35        36        37        38        39
    4Ø        41        42        43        44
    45        46        47        48        49
    5Ø        51        52        53        54
    55        56        57        58        59

Press C to escape, A to alter an entry
or G to go on
```

The procedure for alteration and deletion of entries is similar to that for specimen codes, except that the option to alter name no longer applies, and the program requires three, as opposed to one letter codes.

Option 4 - Alter/Review Antibiotic Names

Select option **4** from the Description File Writer Menu.

```
               DESCRIPTION FILE WRITER

Current antibiotic names are:-

No          Name           No          Name
 Ø    Not used              1    Sulphonamide
 2    Trimethoprim          3    Cotrimoxazole
 4    Ampicillin            5    Gentamicin
 6    Cefuroxime            7    Nalidixate
 8    Nitrofurant           9    Oral Ceph
1Ø    Rifampicin           11    Penicillin
12    Erythromycin         13    Fluclox
14    Fusidic acid         15    Chloramphen
16    Tetracycline         17    Vancomycin
18    Clindamycin          19    Neomycin
2Ø    Spectinomycin        21    Mecillinam
22    Metronidazole        23    Tobramycin
24    Piperacillin         25    Colistin

Press C to escape, A to alter an entry
or G to go on
```

The procedure for altering and erasing these antibiotic names is similar to that already described. NOTE, a printout of this antibiotic name list is essential for work on option 5, Alter/review specimen codes etc.

Option 5 - Alter/Review species codes etc

Select option **5** from the Description File Writer Menu.

```
 1) Name:-                 ??????????
 2) Three letter code:-    ???
 3) 1 letter code:-        ?
 4) Antibiotic  1          Not used
 5) Antibiotic  2          Not used
 6) Antibiotic  3          Not used
 7) Antibiotic  4          Not used
 8) Antibiotic  5          Not used
 9) Antibiotic  6          Not used
1Ø) Antibiotic  7          Not used
11) Antibiotic  8          Not used
12) Antibiotic  9          Not used
13) Antibiotic 1Ø          Not used
14) Antibiotic 11          Not used

Press C to escape, A to alter an entry
or G to go on
```

Press **G** to display the details of the next species.

```
 1) Name:-                 St.aureus
 2) Three letter code:-    sau
 3) 1 letter code:-        s
 4) Antibiotic  1          Penicillin
 5) Antibiotic  2          Fluclox
 6) Antibiotic  3          Fusidic acid
 7) Antibiotic  4          Gentamicin
 8) Antibiotic  5          Chloramphen
 9) Antibiotic  6          Tetracycline
1Ø) Antibiotic  7          Vancomycin
11) Antibiotic  8          Clindamycin
12) Antibiotic  9          Erythromycin
13) Antibiotic 1Ø          Trial 1
14) Antibiotic 11          Trial 2

Press C to escape, A to alter an entry
or G to go on
```

Press **A.** The message changes.

```
Which part do you wish to alter
Press G to go on or type a number (1-14)
and hit RETURN
```

To change the three letter code press **2 RETURN.**

    Enter 3-character code now:*

Enter the new code **QQQ.** The screen is redrawn
with qqq opposite the three letter code, and the
message reverts to 'Which part do you wish to
alter'. To change antibiotic 3, press **6,** the field
number for antibiotic 6, and press **RETURN.** The
message becomes 'Enter the number of the antibiotic
on the list (i.e., $\emptyset$-4$\emptyset$) then press RETURN'.
Look at the antibiotic list printout obtained from
option 4. Antibiotic 2 in the list is
Trimethoprim, type **2** and press **RETURN.** The screen
is redrawn with Trimethoprim in the antibiotic 3
field. To return the details to their original form
alter the three letter code to sau, and antibiotic
three to Fusidic acid (antibiotic 14 in the
antibiotic list).
The user should press **G** for the next species.
Continue to press **G** until the first unfilled
species details are shown. Press **G** once more and
the message 'Would you like a printout of these
codes' appears. Press Y or N.

Options 6, 7 and 8 have been described at the
beginning of this chapter. Password codes may be
modified by similar methods to those described
above.

Advice

The design of the description file is a major
factor in the performance of the programs. The
entry list for each field should include a 'null'
entry to allow for missing or unknown data,
preferably as the first entry of the list. For
example ??? is the first code of the consultant
list. Any list should be written as a series of
related blocks. For example, it would be
advantageous to have all surgical wards in any
hospital in a sequential block in the ward list;
all <u>Enterobacteriaceae</u> in a sequential block in the

species list with, perhaps the enteropathogens as a sub block, and so on. Careful thought and design will allow the very powerful 'Block Select' command to be utilised to its full advantage.

Another trick is to separate blocks with null entries. '?', or '???' in the case of three letter codes, can be entered several times in the list, but the program only uses the first in the programs. Hence, for example, if the consultant list is written in blocks, separated by '???' and a new surgical consultant post is made, the first '???' at the end of the consultant surgeon block can be reassigned to the new consultant.

Note also that fine distinctions can be made between specimen types; if for example the laboratory wishes to distinguish between catheter types then a code can be assigned for each variety in a block. The Block Select command can then be used to lump these together if less fine detail is required. However we would not advise indiscriminate attempts to obtain fine detail; remember the more the operator has to look up codes, the less pleasant data entry becomes.

It is recommended that the user carefully lists the password, specimen type, ward, consultant and species codes which are required for the laboratory and arranges them in suitable order on paper before using the description file writer program. We have found that general discussion and a delay of a few days before writing the file onto the computer helps to ensure that the lists are comprehensive. Modify the current 'sens data' file into the new format, and record the modified file to the description file disk prepared in chapter 3. Ensure that this disk also has an unmodified copy of the dummy data description file for use by others. Now use the description file writer to load your own description file from the description file disk and then record this file on the programs disk as 'sens data', overwriting the dummy data description file. Similarly load your own password file and overwrite the 'codes' file on the programs disk. You are now ready to start entering real data onto your database.

Non-Standard Formats

1) A patient oriented full records system for a specialised unit, eg a Special Care Baby Unit, a Burns Unit or Intensive Care, can be designed. The 'Ward' field could indicate the cot/bed/cubicle in the unit. The 'Consultant' field could be used as a patient identifier, with codes, and therefore patients, a00 to a99 appearing on the first data disks, b00 to b99 on the second and so on. The code list for this field could be left with the program log sheets, and filled out with patient names as the codes are assigned. Specimen types could be assigned as normal, and an extra species code 'nbg', no bacterial growth, added to the species list. This allows the results of all specimens to be recorded for the unit in a file which can be accessed by patient code.

2) For a culture collection database use the specimen type code to indicate the drawer or tray where the culture is stored, specimen number as the collection number, ward code as an indication of source and consultant to indicate special storage/recovery conditions. The 'spp' field would indicate species and the 11 antibiotic fields could indicate month of subculture or biochemical reactions.

3) Serological information may be incorporated by assigning a block of appropriate codes, eg 'fta', in the species code list. The associated antibiotic names could then indicate the dilutions which were positive in serology, r indicating a positive and s a negative result.

These are just a few of the possibilities. A little ingenuity and thought can allow many types of data to be recorded and analysed using these programs.

REFERENCE SECTION

   Each routine is described under numbered
headings in this section. Refer to the index or to
the MICROBE BASE system map to find the appropriate
reference section. System errors and error messages
are detailed in section 7.0

1.0   Loader Routines

1.1   Loading program
   Insert the PROGRAMS disk into the drive with the
label upward and the read window toward the drive
gate. Use the drive labelled 1. Turn on the
printer, monitor and drive.

1.2   Password Entry
   Type in a valid 3-character password when it is
requested. An X is printed in reply to each
keypress. DEL [←] can be used to delete any but
the third character. An invalid password causes the
program to end with an error message.

1.3   Main Microbe Base Menu
   Type a number between 1 and 6 according to the
routine required. Any other keypress will result in
a beep. A logo page appears while the routine is
loaded. Recoverable disk errors occur if no disk or
the wrong disk is in the drive; follow the screen
instructions.

2.0   Entry Routines

NOTE that prime and backup data disks are required in these routines. If they are not available enter an invalid password to leave the program.

2.1   Week Number Entry

From the loader main menu press 1. When the routines are loaded a request for a prime data disk appears. Insert this in drive 1 and press C. Enter a week number between 1 and 52 and press RETURN.

2.2.1 Data Entry - Cursor (*) on left of LNO column

To commence entry of data for an isolate, type a valid specimen type code. To correct the previous isolate data press DEL [←]; the cursor moves to the SENS column of the previous entry to allow editing. To inspect valid code lists or user instructions type * (go to 2.4). To record the data entered on disk, or leave the program if no data has been entered press ^ (go to 2.3). Any other keypress will result in a beep.

2.2.2 Entry of Laboratory Number

Type a number between $\emptyset$ and 99999. If the number has less than 5 digits press RETURN on completion. An incorrect digit can be erased by pressing DEL [←], as can an incorrect specimen code (go to 2.2.1). Any other keypress will result in a beep.

2.2.3 Entry of Ward Code

Type a valid 3 letter ward code. DEL [←] will erase an incorrect letter. If DEL is pressed with the cursor on the left of the column the specimen number will be erased (go to 2.2.2). An invalid code will be erased, returning the cursor to the left of the WRD column after a beep.

2.2.4 Entry of Consultant Code

Type a valid 3 letter consultant code. DEL [←] will erase an incorrect letter. If DEL is pressed with the cursor on the left of the column the ward code will be erased (go to 2.2.3). An invalid code will be erased with a beep, returning the cursor to the left of the CON column.

2.2.5 Entry of Species Code

i) Type a valid 3 letter species code. DEL [←] will erase an incorrect letter. If DEL is pressed with the cursor on the left of the column the consultant code will be erased (go to 2.4). An invalid code will be erased with an error beep, returning the cursor to the left of the SPP column. **OR** ii) Press ↓ [CTRL+B], then enter a valid single character species code. An invalid code will be erased with an error beep, returning the cursor to the left of the SPP column. A valid keypress prints the appropriate 3 letter species code in the SPP column.

2.2.6 Entry of a Susceptibility Pattern

Valid keypresses are:-

i) S, I, U, R or space which print the appropriate character in the current cursor position.

ii) ← [CTRL+A] and → move the cursor left or right without affecting the pattern entered. Attempts to move the cursor beyond the SPP column elicit an error beep and are ignored.

iii) DEL [←] moves the cursor right, substituting a space for the underlying character. DEL will NOT return the cursor to the SPP column.

iv) Open-apple+DEL [CTRL+X] erases the susceptibility pattern and species code entered, returning the cursor to the SPP column.

v) RETURN indicates that the isolate details are correct and moves the cursor to the LNO column on the next line or page (go to 2.1).

2.3 Data Review

The data entered at the current session will be displayed page by page for review. Press C for the next page or W to correct an entry (go to 2.3.1). When all data has been reviewed press R to record (go to 2.3.2) or C to review again (go to 2.3).

2.3.1 Data Correction or Deletion

Enter by pressing W (2.3). The program requests a computer number. Press ^ if no entry is to be corrected, or enter the number in the CNO column of the incorrect entry and press RETURN. Numbers outside the range of the current session will be erased and ignored. The incorrect entry is printed.

Press * to erase the entry completely, or re-enter
the isolate data as in 2.2.1 - 2.2.6 above. The
program returns to the review routines (go to 2.3).

2.3.2 Recording Data to Disk
   Enter by pressing R (2.3). If no data has been
entered, or all data has been deleted the program
ends. Otherwise the program checks that a prime
data disk is in the drive and records the session
entries. Insert a backup data disk when requested.
The program checks the disk and records a copy of
the entries. On completion the computer number
range used is displayed, note this and the date in
the logbook. Press C to return to the Microbe Base
main menu (1.3) or E to end the program.

2.4. Help Menu and Facilities
   With the cursor on the left of the LNO column,
press * (see 2.2.1). The help menu is displayed.
   Press 1 to review the operator instructions.
Insert the programs disk and press C.   The
instructions are displayed. Press C for the next
page or E to end. The program returns to the help
menu.
   Press 2 to review valid codes and details. A
valid data menu is displayed. Press 1-4 to view the
appropriate details, or 5 to return to the help
menu
   Press 3 to return to the entry routines (2.2.1).

3.0   Summary Routines
   NOTE a printer is required in these routines.

3.1   Entry of Selection Criteria
   Press 3 in the loader main menu (1.3) or 1 in
the main recovery menu (4.2), insert the program
disk and press C. After the routines are loaded a
selection menu is printed. Enter the selection
criteria (see pages 51-52). Each line refers to a
particular portion of the record. Possible entries
are:-
   i)   I, signifying Ignore. That portion of the
record will be ignored in selection for analysis.
No printout will be produced for this portion of
the record.
   ii) S, signifying Select, followed by a valid
code. Only records with the code entered will be

selected for analysis. No printout will be produced
for this portion of the record.
 iii) D, signifying Deselect, followed by a valid
code. Only records which do NOT have the code
entered will be selected for analysis. Printout
will be produced for this portion of the record.
 iv) B, signifying Block Select, followed by two
valid codes. This allows the program to select
records with codes between and including the two
codes entered. Refer to your description file
printout; the codes are printed in the order
recognised by Block Select. Printout will be
produced for this portion of the record. Block
Select is NOT a valid command for an antibiotic
field.
 v) C, signifying Count. The program will count
the occurrence of each code for this field in the
records selected, and produce a printout.
 vi) DEL [←] which deletes a letter, code or
command according to cursor position, allowing the
operator to return to previous lines if necessary.
 On completion of the selection criteria, press C
to continue. Ensure that the printer is connected
as requested and press C. The selection criteria
will be printed. Check that the program disk is in
the drive and press C to load the analysis
routines.

3.2   Entry of Search Interval
 After loading the routines the program requests
a data disk. Insert the data disk to be analysed
and press C. The program displays the disk details.
Press C if the disk is to be searched or E if not.
Enter the lowest record number to be inspected and
press RETURN. Enter the highest record number to be
inspected and press RETURN. Incorrect digits can be
erased using DEL [←]; also DEL, pressed in answer
to the request for the highest number, will erase
an incorrect lowest number.
 Check that the printer is connected and press C.
The disk details and search interval will be
printed. The search commences and the computer can
be left unattended. When the search is completed
the program asks if the search is to be extended to
another disk. Further disks can be analysed in a
cumulative search - press Y and insert the next
disk or press N to obtain the search results.

3.3   Summary Printout

Check that the printer is connected and has sufficient paper. NOTE many summaries produce a large printout. Press C and the summary will be printed. A menu is displayed, allowing the user to perform another summary (3.0), return to the main Microbe Base menu (1.3) or end the program.

4.0   Recovery Routines

4.1   Loading Routines

From the Microbe Base main menu (1.3) press 2, check that the program disk is in the drive and press C. When the routines are loaded a menu is displayed.

4.2   Main Recovery Menu

Press a number from 1-8 according to the routine required. All other keypresses elicit an error beep.

4.2.1 Obtain a Summary

From the main recovery menu press 1. Insert the programs disk and press C as requested. The routines are loaded. Go to section 3.0

4.2.2 Print Results to Printer

From the main recovery menu press 2. Insert the data disk as requested and press C. The disk details are displayed; press C to continue. Enter the lowest computer record number required. The program will accept numeric keypresses, DEL [←], which deletes the last digit entered, and RETURN, which indicates completion of the number. Enter the highest record computer number required as above; DEL [←] pressed when no digits have been entered allows re-entry of the lowest record number. Ensure that the printer is connected and press any key. The isolate records in the range specified are printed, with the specimen type and species as full names rather than codes. To abort printing prior to completion of the search press E; press C to continue on completion of a full search. The program reverts to the main recovery menu (4.2).

4.2.3 Leaf Through Results

From the main recovery menu press 3. Insert the data disk as requested and press C. The disk details are displayed; press C to continue. Enter the lowest record computer number required. The program will accept numeric keypresses, DEL [←], which deletes the last digit entered, and RETURN, which indicates completion of the number. Enter the highest record computer number required as above; DEL [←] pressed when no digits have been entered allows re-entry of the lowest record number. The isolate records in the range specified are displayed 20 at a time. To abort the search prior to completion press E, or press C to display the next 20 records until the search is complete. Press any key, the program reverts to the main recovery menu (4.2).

4.2.4 Selective Leaf Through

From the main recovery menu press 4. Insert the data disk as requested and press C. The disk details are displayed; press C to continue. Enter the lowest record computer number required. The program will accept numeric keypresses, DEL [←], which deletes the last digit entered, and RETURN, which indicates completion of the number. Enter the highest record computer number required as above; DEL [←] pressed when no digits have been entered allows re-entry of the lowest record number. The selection criteria menu is displayed, with the cursor on the line 'Specimen type'. Valid entries are:-

i) I, indicating Ignore, which removes the specimen type from consideration in selecting records to display.

ii) S, indicating Select, followed by a valid specimen code which specifies that only records with the code entered will be displayed.

iii) D, indicating Deselect, followed by a valid specimen code which specifies that only records which do NOT have the code entered will be displayed.

iv) B, indicating Block Select, followed by two valid specimen codes. This specifies that only records with a code the same as either of the codes entered or between these two codes in the specimen code list will be displayed. NOTE Block Select is

not accepted for an antibiotic field.
 v)   DEL [<--] which will delete the last keypress
or last complete entry.
    Specify the search criterion for each successive
field; antibiotic fields accept S, I, U, R or Space
as valid codes. Press any key to continue, then
press 1 to display records to screen or 2 to print
records to printer.
    If the printer option is specified ensure that
the printer is connected and press C; the records
complying with the search criteria are printed as
outlined in 4.2.2 above. Selection of the screen
option displays records complying with the search
criteria in the range specified 20 at a time as in
4.2.3 above. To abort the search prior to
completion press E, or press C to display the next
20 records until the search is complete. Press any
key, the program reverts to the main recovery menu
(4.2).

4.2.5 Search for a Result on a Specimen
    From the main recovery menu press 5. Insert a
data disk and press C to display the disk details.
Specify the lowest and highest computer record
numbers to search as detailed in 4.2.3. Enter the
specimen type code and laboratory number of the
record required and press RETURN. If isolate
records with the number and specimen code specified
are found they are displayed on the screen. Press E
to abort the search or C to revert to the main
recovery menu (4.2) on search completion.

4.2.6 Operator Instructions
    From the main recovery menu press 6. Insert the
programs disk as requested and press C.   The
operator instructions are displayed a page at a
time. Press C for the next page or E to return to
the main recovery menu (4.2).

4.2.7 Valid Entry Tables
    From the main recovery menu press 7. The valid
entry menu is displayed. To review specimen type,
ward and consultant codes or species coding details
press the appropriate number. Appropriate codes and
details are displayed; press C or E as indicated,
on completion of the review of the details selected
the program reverts to the main recovery menu

(4.2).

4.2.8 End Recovery Routines
   From the main menu press 8, remove the disk and
press C to return to the Microbe Base main menu
(1.3) or E to end the program.

5.0   Disk Handling Routines

5.1   Loading Routines
   Press 4 in the Microbe Base main menu (1.3) and
press C. After the routines are loaded the disk
handling menu is displayed. Press a numeric key 1-7
according to the routine required. Other keypresses
are ignored.

5.1.1 Alter Disk Status
   Press 1 in the disk handling menu. Insert a data
disk and press C. The program checks that it is a
data disk.
   If the disk is a data disk its details are
printed. Press P, B or A according to the disk
status required. The status is altered and the disk
handling menu displayed (5.1).

5.1.2 Alter Disk Maximum Number
   Press 2 in the disk handling menu. Insert a data
disk and press C. The program checks that it is a
data disk.
   If the disk is a data disk its details are
printed. Enter the new maximum number and press
RETURN. NOTE records with computer numbers greater
than the number entered will no longer be accessed
by recovery or summary routines and each further
entry of isolate data will overwrite one
unaccessible record. This can be used to re-enter
an incorrect entry; the previous maximum number can
then be reinstated, allowing access to the full
records. NOTE that both the prime and backup disk
should be altered if this is attempted. The maximum
number is altered and the disk handling menu
displayed (5.1).

5.1.3 Format a Data Disk
   Press 3 in the disk handling menu. Insert a NEW
unformatted disk and press C. NOTE THE DISK WILL BE
OVERWRITTEN, ANY DATA OR PROGRAMS WILL BE ERASED.

Enter a title for the disk; incorrect characters can be erased by pressing DEL [<-], then press RETURN. The program gives a final opportunity to revert to the menu (press E). Press C to format the disk. The drive runs for 1 minute; the disk is checked for faults, formatted and given ARCHIVE status. The program confirms that formatting was successful. Press C to revert to the disk handling menu (5.1).

5.1.4 Format a Description List Disk
    Press 4 in the disk handling menu. Insert a NEW unformatted disk and press C. NOTE THE DISK WILL BE OVERWRITTEN, ANY DATA OR PROGRAMS WILL BE ERASED. Enter a title for the disk, incorrect characters can be erased by pressing DEL [<-], then press RETURN. The program gives a final opportunity to revert to the menu (press E). Press C to format the disk. The drive runs for 1 minute. The program confirms the title. Press C to revert to the disk handling menu (5.1).

5.1.5 Archive 1200 records from a Data Disk
    NOTE the data disk to be archived must have 1200 records and the data disk to which the records are to be transferred must have 8401 records.
    Press 5 in the disk handling menu. Insert the programs disk as requested and press C. Press 1 RETURN if a single disk drive is connected or 2 RETURN for a dual drive. When the routines have been loaded insert the data disk to be archived and press C. The disk details are displayed. Press Y if the disk is to be archived, N to end. Insert the data disk to which the records are to be transferred and press C. The disk details are displayed. Press Y to transfer the data or N to end. The program asks for the 'sender' disk; insert this and press C. The drive runs for 4 minutes and asks for the 'receiver' disk. Insert this and press C. The drive runs for 4 minutes and the records 1-1200 from the sender are recorded to the receiver. The sender disk is requested, insert this and press C. The drive runs for several minutes. Records 1-1200 are erased and all higher records numbers are lowered by 1200. Archive both prime and backup disks at the same session, and note the

change in record numbers in the logbook.
    NOTE archiving differs in detail when a dual disk drive is used and takes less time. Simply follow the screen instructions.

5.1.6 Copy a Data Disk
    Press 6 in the disk handling menu. Insert the programs disk as requested and press C. Press 1 RETURN if a single disk drive is connected or 2 RETURN for a dual drive . When the routines and data have been loaded insert the data disk to be copied and press C. The disk details are displayed. Press Y if the disk is to be copied, N to end. Insert the data disk to which the records are to be transferred and press C. The disk details are displayed. Press Y to transfer the data or N to end. NOTE IF Y IS PRESSED THIS DISK WILL BE OVERWRITTEN, ERASING ALL DATA OR PROGRAMS. The program asks for the 'sender' disk; insert this and press C. The drive runs for 4 minutes and asks for the 'receiver' disk. Insert this and press C. The drive runs for 4 minutes and the records 1-1200 from the sender are recorded to the receiver. The program then requests further similar cycles until all records have been copied.
    NOTE copying differs in detail when a dual disk drive is used and takes less time. Simply follow the screen instructions.

5.1.7 End Program
    Press 7 in the disk handling menu. Remove the disk as requested and press C to return to the Microbe Base main menu (1.3) or E to end.

6.0   Description File Editor
    NOTE the programs use the description file entitled 'sens data' and password file 'codes' on the programs disk. These are the only data files recognised as valid by routines other than the description file editor. The editor can, however, transfer description and password files to the programs disk from a description file disk and vice-versa. This allows the programs to operate several independent records systems, each with its own logbook, description and password files and set of prime, archive and backup disks. When description and password files are transferred and

overwritten ensure that copies are retained on the description file disk. THE PROGRAMS DO NOT CHECK THAT A COPY HAS BEEN RETAINED.

6.1   Loading Routines
Press 5 in the main loader menu. The routines are loaded.

6.2   Load Description File to be Edited
A page describing the functions of the program is displayed. Press any key; the description file menu is displayed. Some of the menu options will require that a description file be loaded. In this case insert the disk with a copy of the description file to be edited/transferred and press C. The program requests the title of the description file. Type this and press RETURN; DEL [←] can be used to delete erroneous characters. The drive searches for the file and loads the data. An error message is given if the file is nor present and the program reverts to the description file menu.

6.3   Description File Menu
The description file menu is displayed. Press a number 1-9 according to the routine required.

6.3.1 Alter/Review Specimen Codes
From the description writer menu press 1. The first 25 list numbers, specimen codes and specimen names are displayed. Press C to return to the menu, A to alter/delete a code/name or G to display details of the next 25 codes. If A is pressed the list number is requested. Press C if no correction was required or type a list number and press RETURN; DEL [←] can be used to delete an incorrect digit. If the number entered corresponds to the last entry in the list you will be asked if you wish to erase the entry. Otherwise you will be given an opportunity to to alter the 1-letter code and/or the specimen name. Press a single key to enter a code or up to 15 characters followed by RETURN to enter a name. NOTE ONLY THE LAST FILLED ENTRY IN THE LIST CAN BE ERASED ALSO ⌃ AND * ARE NOT VALID SPECIMEN CODES. When all codes have been reviewed press Y to obtain a printout or N to revert to the description writer menu.

6.3.2 Alter/Review Ward Codes

From the description writer menu press 2. The first 60 list numbers and ward codes are displayed. Press C to return to the menu, A to alter/delete a code or G to display details of the next 60 codes. If A is pressed the list number is requested. Press C if no correction was required or type a list number and press RETURN; DEL [<-] can be used to delete an incorrect digit. If the entered number corresponds to the last entry in the list you will be given an opportunity to erase the entry. If a code is to be altered type the new 3 letter code. NOTE ONLY THE LAST FILLED ENTRY IN THE LIST CAN BE ERASED. When all codes have been reviewed press Y to obtain a printout or N to revert to the description writer menu (6.3).

6.3.3 Alter/Review Consultant Codes

From the description writer menu press 3. The first 60 list numbers and consultant codes are displayed. Press C to return to the menu, A to alter/delete a code or G to display details of the next 60 codes. If A is pressed the list number is requested. Press C if no correction was required or type a list number and press RETURN; DEL [<-] can be used to delete an incorrect digit. If the entered number corresponds to the last entry in the list you will be given an opportunity to erase the entry. If a code is to be altered type the new 3 letter code. NOTE ONLY THE LAST FILLED ENTRY IN THE LIST CAN BE ERASED. When all codes have been reviewed press Y to obtain a printout or N to revert to the description writer menu (6.3).

6.3.4 Alter/Review Antibiotic Names

From the description writer menu press 4. The first 25 list numbers and antibiotic names are displayed. Press C to return to the main menu, A to alter/delete a name or G to display details of the next 25 names. If A is pressed the list number is requested. Press C if no correction was required or type a list number and press RETURN; DEL [<-] can be used to delete an incorrect digit. If the entered number corresponds to the last entry in the list you will be given an opportunity to erase the entry. If a name is to be altered type the new name consisting of up to 12 letters and press RETURN.

NOTE ONLY THE LAST FILLED ENTRY IN THE LIST CAN BE
ERASED. When all codes have been reviewed press Y
to obtain a printout or N to revert to the
description writer menu (6.3). NOTE A PRINTOUT OF
THE ANTIBIOTIC NAME LIST IS ESSENTIAL IN EDITING
SPECIES DETAILS.

6.3.5 Alter/Review Species Details

    From the description writer menu press 5. The
name, 3 letter code, 1 letter code and names of the
11 antibiotics specified are displayed for the
first species entry. A field number is displayed as
a bracketed number on the left of each screen line.
Press C to return to the menu, A to alter/delete
details or G to display details of the next
species. If A is pressed a field number is
requested. Press C if no correction was required or
type the number of the field to be altered and
press RETURN; DEL can be used to delete   an
incorrect digit. NOTE ONLY THE LAST FILLED ENTRY IN
THE LIST CAN BE ERASED. Type the corrected entry -
3 letters for a 3 letter code; any printed
character, including shifted characters, for a 1
letter code; up to 15 letters for a species name;
or the list number of the appropriate antibiotic
obtained from a printout of antibiotic names. To
add a new species, press G until you see the first
blank entry - ie an entry with no species name or
1- or 3-letter codes, then modify this
appropriately. When all species details have been
reviewed press Y to obtain a printout or N to
revert to the description file menu (6.3).

6.3.6 Record Description File

    From the description writer menu press 6. Insert
the disk on which the description file is to be
recorded and press C to continue or E to revert to
the description writer menu. Enter a file name of
up to 30 characters and press RETURN; any character
except a comma may be used, but the first character
must be a letter. DEL [<-] may be used to delete
erroneous keypresses. The program checks for the
presence of a file with the same name; if there is
none then the description file is recorded. If a
file with the same name exists on the disk the
program asks if it should be overwritten. Press O
to record the file under this name, or E to return

to the description file menu. NOTE THE ORIGINAL
VERSION OF AN OVERWRITTEN FILE WILL BE ERASED, DO
YOU HAVE A BACKUP COPY? The only description file
recognised by routines other than description file
writer is that named 'sens data' on the programs
disk. Files can be renamed/exchanged from the
description file disk to the programs disk by
entering the appropriate disk and name in 6.2 above
to pick up the file, and use of option 6 from the
description writer menu to record it on another
disk and/or another name.

6.3.7 Alter/Review Password File

   From the description writer menu press 7. If the
password file has not already been loaded you will
be prompted to load it. In this case insert the
disk with the password file required and press C to
continue. Enter the password file name of up to 30
characters and press RETURN; DEL [←] may be used
to delete erroneous keypresses. The program checks
for the presence of a file with this name and loads
the data or gives an error message and returns to
the description writer menu. The list of passwords
is displayed. Press C to return to the menu, A to
alter a password, or G to return to the description
file menu (6.3). Enter the number of the password
to be altered and type a 3 letter password. Only
the last filled entry can be erased.

6.3.8 Record Password File

   From the description writer menu press 8. Insert
the disk on which the password file is to be
recorded and press C to continue or E to revert to
the description writer menu. Enter a file name of
up to 30 characters and press RETURN; any character
except a comma may be used, but the first character
must be a letter. DEL [←] may be used to delete
erroneous keypresses. The program checks for the
presence of a file with the same name; if there is
none then the password file is recorded. If a file
with the same name exists on the disk the program
asks if it should be overwritten. Press O to record
the file under this name, or E to return to the
description file menu. NOTE THE ORIGINAL VERSION OF
AN OVERWRITTEN FILE WILL BE ERASED, DO YOU HAVE A
BACKUP COPY?. The only password file recognised by
routines other than description file writer is that

named 'codes' on the programs disk. Files can be renamed/exchanged from the description file disk to the programs disk by entering the appropriate disk and name in 6.3.7 above to pick up the file, and use of option 8 from the description writer menu to record it on another disk and/or another name.

6.3.9 End Program

NOTE - RECORD THE EDITED DESCRIPTION OR PASSWORD FILE TO DISK OR ALL EDITS WILL BE LOST. Option 9 gives you a final opportunity to do this before ending the program. Remove the disk from the drive and press C to return to the Microbe Base main menu (1.3) or E to end the program.

7.0   Error Messages

Most errors elicit a beep and the erroneous entry is ignored; some produce an error message giving instructions on how to proceed; very few produce an irrecoverable error and all of these are associated with damage to the disks. Careful attention to the points outlined in Precautions and Advice should prevent these problems. Frequent occurrence of this type of error indicate a hardware malfunction, unfiltered fluctuations or spikes on the electricity supply, or that the disks are being mis-handled.

On occurrence of an irretrievable error or if an emergency shutdown of the programs is required simply switch off the computer and printer.

NOTE the programs may occasionally fail to respond to keypresses for a period of up to 30 seconds. This tends to occur in the longer programs such as the description file writer and does not indicate a malfunction. The computer is re-arranging memory allocation.

The error message 'I can't find the file I want' usually occurs when the programs fail to find the description and password files 'sens data' and 'codes'. This usually indicates an incorrect disk in the drive. Check that it is the programs disk. If it is then end the program and attempt to rewrite these files from backup copies using the description file writer. Otherwise insert the programs disk and press C.

Two types of record error may occasionally be found when the recovery or summary routines are

used, neither affects program operation. 'Bad
Record at xxxx' indicates that the record with
computer number xxxx has an invalid code or
susceptibility pattern; a record of this type
exists on the demonstration data disks. This is
normally generated as a result of deleting codes
from the description file. These records may be
correctly reinstated using the procedure outlined
on pages 59-60. 'NO RECORD HERE' indicates that the
maximum record number was set higher than the
actual number of records on the disk. Use the
procedures on pages 59-60 to reset the maximum
record number to the correct value.

MICROBE BASE SYSTEM MAP

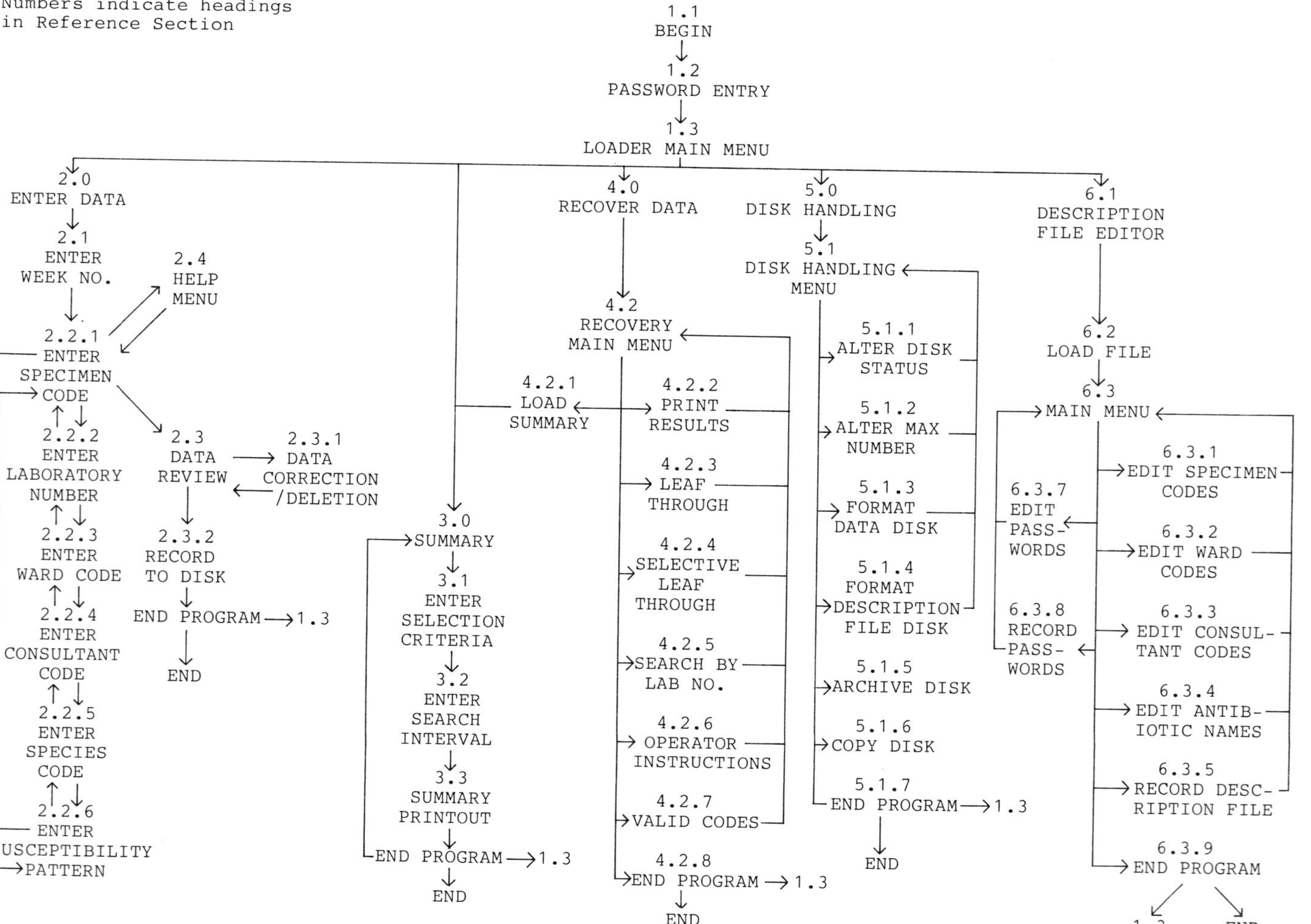

Apple IIc/e and Apple II+ Keypresses

FUNCTION	IIe/IIc	II+
Delete previous character	DEL	←
Non-destructive backspace	←	CTRL+A
Cursor right	→	→ or CTRL+S
Delete species entry	open-apple+DEL	CTRL+X
One character species entry	↓	CTRL+B

APPENDIX

LOG SHEET FOR DUMMY DATA BASE

Data base operating-   Routine sensitivities
group lab

Prime data disk   -   microbe base p
Backup data disk   -   microbe base b

Date	Start Session		End Session		Operator
	Spec No	Comp No	Spec No	Comp No	
Week 1					
2nd Jan 84	x119	1	p13	50	JTM
3rd Jan 84	p15	51	p9	100	PFW
4th Jan 84	p10	101	w87	147	PFW
5th Jan 84	u295	148	w95	202	JTM
6th Jan 84	w97	203	b115	247	PFW
Week 2					
9th Jan 84	b120	248	w192	307	PFW
10th Jan 84	w195	308	h120	350	JTM
11th Jan 84	h125	351	u759	402	PFW
12th Jan 84	u762	403	s159	451	PFW
13th Jan 84	s162	452	w247	505	JTM

NB Consultant sic left, replaced by saw, code
altered from this point.

Date	Start Session		End Session		Operator
Week 3					
16th Jan 84	w249	506	u869	559	PFW
17th Jan 84	u870	560	e97	602	PFW
18th Jan 84	e98	603	w347	647	JTM
19th Jan 84	g130	648	w366	701	PFW
20th Jan 84	u1000	702	x97	749	JTM
Week 4					
23rd Jan 84	m25	750	g139	759	PFW
24th Jan 84	g142	760	u1137	802	PFW
25th Jan 84	u1137	803	u1207	847	JTM
26th Jan 84	u1208	848	u1300	901	PFW
27th Jan 84	u1306	902	b352	949	JTM

```
Week 5
30th Jan 84    b355      950      u70    1005    PFW
31st Jan 84    u71      1006      p2     1062    PFW
 1st Feb 84    p4       1063      w53    1107    JTM
 2nd Feb 84    w60      1108      u260   1151    PFW
 3rd Feb 84    u290     1152      w92    1209    JTM

Week 6
 6th Feb 84    s52      1210      b102   1255    PFW
 7th Feb 84    b103     1256      w125   1302    PFW
 8th Feb 84    w128     1303      b192   1357    JTM
 9th Feb 84    b193     1358      u537   1401    PFW
10th Feb 84    u538     1402      w227   1459    JTM

Week 7
13th Feb 84    p34      1460      x69    1505    PFW
14th Feb 84    x70      1506      w252   1552    PFW
15th Feb 84    w257     1553      u874   1607    JTM
16th Feb 84    u875     1608      w306   1651    PFW
17th Feb 84    w309     1652      u965   1709    JTM

Week 8
20th Feb 84    u972     1710      u1025  1755    PFW
21st Feb 84    u1027    1756      w389   1802    PFW
22nd Feb 84    g139     1803      u1163  1857    JTM
23rd Feb 84    u1165    1858      g165   1901    PFW
24th Feb 84    g166     1902      u1345  2000    JTM
```

DESCRIPTION FILE FOR DUMMY DATA BASE

1) Valid Specimen Site Codes:-

0	?	not known	1	u	catch urine
2	t	csu	3	w	wound swab
4	b	blood culture	5	s	sputum
6	g	genital swab	7	c	csf
8	f	faeces	9	m	pm tissue
10	p	pus	11	a	aspirate
12	d	capd fluid	13	v	valve/shunt
14	e	ear swab	15	y	eye swab
16	n	nose swab	17	h	throat swab
18	x	enviromental	19	z	tissue

2) Valid Ward & Department Codes

a) Wards

0	???	Null Entry	1	??g	? Origin
2	1ag		3	1bg	
4	2ag		5	2bg	
6	3ag		7	3bg	
8	4ag		9	4bg	
10	5ag		11	5ag	
12	6ag		13	6bg	
14	7ag		15	7bg	
16	8ag		17	8bg	
18	9ag		19	icg	Intensive Care
20	ccg	Coronary Care	21	rtg	Renal Transplant
22	thg	Theatres	23	occ	Occ. Health
24	??p	? Origin	25	w1p	
26	w2p		27	w3p	
28	w4p		29	w5p	
30	w6p		31	icp	Intensive Care
32	isp	Isolation	33	thp	Theatres
34	??b	? Origin	35	jsb	John Smith Ward
36	jtb	Josh Tetley Ward	37	ssb	Sam Smith Ward
38	jcb	J. Courage Ward	39	thb	Theatres
40	?og	? o/p	41	aeg	Acc/Emergency
42	sog	Surgical o/p	43	org	Ortho o/p
44	mog	Medical o/p	45	gpg	Gen.Pract
46	dwg	Day Ward	47	eng	ENT o/p
48	ang	Ante-Natal	49	uog	Urology o/p
50	hag	Haematology o/p	51	pag	Pathology
52	gog	Gynae o/p	53	dug	Dialysis unit
54	deg	Dermatology o/p	55	opg	Ophthalmic o/p
56	bog	Burns o/p	57	rog	Renal o/p
58	gud	Genito-Urin Med	59	?op	? o/p
60	aep	Acc/Emergency	61	sop	Surgical o/p
62	orp	Ortho o/p	63	mop	Medical o/p
64	gpp	Gen.Pract	65	dwp	Day Ward
66	enp	ENT o/p	67	hap	Haematology o/p
68	pap	Surgical o/p			

3) Consultant Codes

0	???	Unknown	1	cut	Surgeon
2	sew	Surgeon	3	hac	Surgeon
4	dia	Physician	5	puo	Physician
6	sbe	Physician	7	nut	Neurosurgeon
8	rta	NeuroSurgeon	9	wee	Renal
10	uti	Renal Consultant	11	nsu	GU Physician
12	pid	GU Physician	13	obs	Obs Consult
14	see	Ophth Consultant	15	saw	Ortho Surgeon
16	hip	Ortho Surgeon	17	cap	Ortho Surgeon
18	kid	Paediatrician	19	tot	Paediatrician
20	nip	Paediatrician	21	bts	Haematologist
22	fbc	Haematologist	23	gas	Anaesthetist
24	blo	Anaesthetist	25	doa	Pathologist
26	ded	Pathologist	26	gyn	Gynaecologist
28	tab	ENT Consultant			

4) Antibiotic List

No	Antibiotic	No	Antibiotic	No	Antibiotic
1	Sulphonamide	15	Chloramphen	28	5 F Cytosine
2	Trimethoprim	16	Tetracycline	29	Miconazole
3	Cotrimoxazol	17	Vancomycin	30	Cephtizoxime
4	Ampicillin	18	Clindamycin	31	Amikacin
5	Gentamicin	19	Neomycin	32	Trial 1
6	Cefuroxime	20	Spectino	33	Trial 2
7	Nalidixate	21	Mecillinam	34	Streptomycin
8	Nitrofurant	22	Metronidazol	35	PAS
9	Oral Ceph	23	Tobramycin	36	Isoniazid
10	Rifampicin	24	Piperacillin	37	Ethambutol
11	Penicillin	25	Colistin	38	Pyrazinamide
12	Erythromycin	26	Nystatin	39	Ethionamide
13	Fluclox	27	Amphotericin	40	Cycloserine
14	Fusidic acid				

5) Valid Species List

a)Gram Positive Cocci

```
Species name   . St.aureus          . St.epidermidis .   Strep Grp A       .
Code 3 letter  . sau                . sep            .   sga               .
Code 1 letter  . s                  . E              .   A                 .
Antibiotic  1  . Penicillin   (11)  . Penicillin  (11)  . Penicillin   (11)  .
Antibiotic  2  . Fluclox      (13)  . Fluclox     (13)  . Erythromycin (12)  .
Antibiotic  3  . Fusidic acid (14)  . Fusidic acid (14) . Tetracycline (16)  .
Antibiotic  4  . Gentamicin   ( 5)  . Gentamicin  ( 5)  . Cotrimoxazol ( 3)  .
Antibiotic  5  . Chloramphen  (15)  . Chloramphen (15)  . Chloramphen  (15)  .
Antibiotic  6  . Tetracycline (16)  . Tetracycline (16) . Not used     ( 0)  .
Antibiotic  7  . Vancomycin   (17)  . Vancomycin  (17)  . Not used     ( 0)  .
Antibiotic  8  . Clindamycin  (18)  . Clindamycin (18)  . Not used     ( 0)  .
Antibiotic  9  . Erythromycin (12)  . Erythromycin (12) . Not used     ( 0)  .
Antibiotic 10  . Trial 1      (32)  . Trial 1     (32)  . Trial 1      (32)  .
Antibiotic 11  . Trial 2      (33)  . Trial 2     (33)  . Trial 2      (33)  .


Species name   . Strep Grp B        . Strep Grp C      . Strep Grp F       .
Code 3 letter  . sgb                . sgc              . sgf               .
Code 1 letter  . B                  . C                . F                 .
Antibiotic  1  . Penicillin   (11)  . Penicillin  (11)  . Penicillin   (11)  .
Antibiotic  2  . Erythromycin (12)  . Erythromycin (12) . Erythromycin (12)  .
Antibiotic  3  . Tetracycline (16)  . Tetracycline (16) . Tetracycline (16)  .
Antibiotic  4  . Cotrimoxazol ( 3)  . Cotrimoxazol ( 3) . Cotrimoxazol ( 3)  .
Antibiotic  5  . Chloramphen  (15)  . Chloramphen (15)  . Chloramphen  (15)  .
Antibiotic  6  . Not used     ( 0)  . Not used    ( 0)  . Not used     ( 0)  .
Antibiotic  7  . Not used     ( 0)  . Not used    ( 0)  . Not used     ( 0)  .
Antibiotic  8  . Not used     ( 0)  . Not used    ( 0)  . Not used     ( 0)  .
Antibiotic  9  . Not used     ( 0)  . Not used    ( 0)  . Not used     ( 0)  .
Antibiotic 10  . Trial 1      (32)  . Trial 1     (32)  . Trial 1      (32)  .
Antibiotic 11  . Trial 2      (33)  . Trial 2     (33)  . Trial 2      (33)  .


Species name   . Strep Grp G        . Strep Not Grpd  . Alpha H Strep     .
Code 3 letter  . sgg                . sng              . ahs               .
Code 1 letter  . G                  . 1                . 2                 .
Antibiotic  1  . Penicillin   (11)  . Penicillin  (11)  . Penicillin   (11)  .
Antibiotic  2  . Erythromycin (12)  . Erythromycin (12) . Erythromycin (12)  .
Antibiotic  3  . Tetracycline (16)  . Tetracycline (16) . Tetracycline (16)  .
Antibiotic  4  . Cotrimoxazol ( 3)  . Cotrimoxazol ( 3) . Cotrimoxazol ( 3)  .
Antibiotic  5  . Chloramphen  (15)  . Chloramphen (15)  . Chloramphen  (15)  .
Antibiotic  6  . Not used     ( 0)  . Not used    ( 0)  . Not used     ( 0)  .
Antibiotic  7  . Not used     ( 0)  . Not used    ( 0)  . Not used     ( 0)  .
Antibiotic  8  . Not used     ( 0)  . Not used    ( 0)  . Not used     ( 0)  .
Antibiotic  9  . Not used     ( 0)  . Not used    ( 0)  . Not used     ( 0)  .
Antibiotic 10  . Trial 1      (32)  . Trial 1     (32)  . Trial 1      (32)  .
Antibiotic 11  . Trial 2      (33)  . Trial 2     (33)  . Trial 2      (33)  .
```

```
Species name   .   Non H Strep      .   Str. pneumoniae.    Str. faecalis   .
Code 3 letter  .   nhs              .   spn             .   sfa             .
Code 1 letter  .   3                .   4               .   D               .
Antibiotic  1 . Penicillin   (11) . Penicillin   (11) . Ampicillin   ( 4) .
Antibiotic  2 . Erythromycin (12) . Erythromycin (12) . Erythromycin (12) .
Antibiotic  3 . Tetracycline (16) . Tetracycline (16) . Tetracycline (16) .
Antibiotic  4 . Cotrimoxazol ( 3) . Cotrimoxazol ( 3) . Cotrimoxazol ( 3) .
Antibiotic  5 . Chloramphen  (15) . Chloramphen  (15) . Chloramphen  (15) .
Antibiotic  6 . Not used     ( 0) . Not used     ( 0) . Nitrofurant  ( 8) .
Antibiotic  7 . Not used     ( 0) . Not used     ( 0) . Not used     ( 0) .
Antibiotic  8 . Not used     ( 0) . Not used     ( 0) . Not used     ( 0) .
Antibiotic  9 . Not used     ( 0) . Not used     ( 0) . Not used     ( 0) .
Antibiotic 10 . Trial 1      (32) . Trial 1      (32) . Trial 1      (32) .
Antibiotic 11 . Trial 2      (33) . Trial 2      (33) . Trial 2      (33) .


Species name   .   Branhamella      .   Anaerobic cocci.
Code 3 letter  .   bra              .   aco             .
Code 1 letter  .   5                .   6               .
Antibiotic  1 . Penicillin   (11) . Penicillin   (11) .
Antibiotic  2 . Erythromycin (12) . Erythromycin (12) .
Antibiotic  3 . Tetracycline (16) . Tetracycline (16) .
Antibiotic  4 . Cotrimoxazol ( 3) . Metronidazol (22) .
Antibiotic  5 . Ampicillin   ( 4) . Chloramphen  (15) .
Antibiotic  6 . Not used     ( 0) . Not used     ( 0) .
Antibiotic  7 . Not used     ( 0) . Not used     ( 0) .
Antibiotic  8 . Not used     ( 0) . Not used     ( 0) .
Antibiotic  9 . Not used     ( 0) . Not used     ( 0) .
Antibiotic 10 . Trial 1      (32) . Trial 1      (32) .
Antibiotic 11 . Trial 2      (33) . Trial 2      (33) .
```

b) Gram Positive Bacilli

```
Species name   .   Diphtheroid      .   Listeria        .   Erysipelothrix .
Code 3 letter  .   dip              .   lis             .   ery            .
Code 1 letter  .   '                .   l               .   +              .
Antibiotic  1 . Penicillin   (11) . Penicillin   (11) . Penicillin   (11) .
Antibiotic  2 . Erythromycin (12) . Erythromycin (12) . Erythromycin (12) .
Antibiotic  3 . Tetracycline (16) . Tetracycline (16) . Tetracycline (16) .
Antibiotic  4 . Cotrimoxazol ( 3) . Cotrimoxazol ( 3) . Cotrimoxazol ( 3) .
Antibiotic  5 . Chloramphen  (15) . Chloramphen  (15) . Chloramphen  (15) .
Antibiotic  6 . Not used     ( 0) . Ampicillin   ( 4) . Ampicillin   ( 4) .
Antibiotic  7 . Not used     ( 0) . Not used     ( 0) . Not used     ( 0) .
Antibiotic  8 . Not used     ( 0) . Not used     ( 0) . Not used     ( 0) .
Antibiotic  9 . Not used     ( 0) . Not used     ( 0) . Not used     ( 0) .
Antibiotic 10 . Trial 1      (32) . Trial 1      (32) . Trial 1      (32) .
Antibiotic 11 . Trial 2      (33) . Trial 2      (33) . Trial 2      (33) .
```

```
Species name  .    Aerobic sporer .    C.perfringens  .    Clostridia      .
Code 3 letter .    asb             .    cpe            .    clo             .
Code 1 letter .    a               .    W              .    Z               .
Antibiotic  1 . Penicillin   (11) . Penicillin   (11) . Penicillin   (11) .
Antibiotic  2 . Erythromycin (12) . Erythromycin (12) . Erythromycin (12) .
Antibiotic  3 . Tetracycline (16) . Clindamycin  (18) . Clindamycin  (18) .
Antibiotic  4 . Not used    ( 0) . Metronidazol (22) . Metronidazol (22) .
Antibiotic  5 . Not used    ( 0) . Not used    ( 0) . Not used    ( 0) .
Antibiotic  6 . Not used    ( 0) . Not used    ( 0) . Not used    ( 0) .
Antibiotic  7 . Not used    ( 0) . Not used    ( 0) . Not used    ( 0) .
Antibiotic  8 . Not used    ( 0) . Not used    ( 0) . Not used    ( 0) .
Antibiotic  9 . Not used    ( 0) . Not used    ( 0) . Not used    ( 0) .
Antibiotic 10 . Trial 1     (32) . Trial 1     (32) . Trial 1     (32) .
Antibiotic 11 . Trial 2     (33) . Trial 2     (33) . Trial 2     (33) .


Species name  .    Actinomyces     .    M.tuberculosis .    Mycobacteria    .
Code 3 letter .    act             .    mtu            .    myc             .
Code 1 letter .    @               .    #              .    -               .
Antibiotic  1 . Penicillin   (11) . Streptomycin (34) . Sreptomycin  (34) .
Antibiotic  2 . Erythromycin (12) . PAS          (35) . PAS          (35) .
Antibiotic  3 . Tetracycline (16) . Isoniazid    (36) . Isoniazid    (36) .
Antibiotic  4 . Cotrimoxazol ( 3) . Ethambutol   (37) . Ethambutol   (37) .
Antibiotic  5 . Fluclox      (13) . Pyrazinamide (38) . Pyrazinamide (38) .
Antibiotic  6 . Sulphonamide ( 1) . Ethionamide  (39) . Ethionamide  (39) .
Antibiotic  7 . Not used    ( 0) . Cycloserine  (40) . Cycloserine  (40) .
Antibiotic  8 . Not used    ( 0) . Not used    ( 0) . Not used    ( 0) .
Antibiotic  9 . Not used    ( 0) . Not used    ( 0) . Not used    ( 0) .
Antibiotic 10 . Trial 1     (32) . Trial 1     (32) . Trial 1     (32) .
Antibiotic 11 . Trial 2     (33) . Trial 2     (33) . Trial 2     (33) .
```

c) Gram Negative Cocci

```
Species name  .    N.meningitidis .    N.gonorrhoeae  .    Viellonella     .
Code 3 letter .    nme            .    ngo            .    vie             .
Code 1 letter .    &              .    $              .    %               .
Antibiotic  1 . Penicillin   (11) . Penicillin   (11) . Penicillin   (11) .
Antibiotic  2 . Erythromycin (12) . Erythromycin (12) . Erythromycin (12) .
Antibiotic  3 . Tetracycline (16) . Spectino     (20) . Tetracycline (16) .
Antibiotic  4 . Sulphonamide ( 1) . Ceftizoxime  (30) . Metronidazol (22) .
Antibiotic  5 . Chloramphen  (15) . Not used    ( 0) . Not used    ( 0) .
Antibiotic  6 . Rifampicin   (10) . Not used    ( 0) . Not used    ( 0) .
Antibiotic  7 . Not used    ( 0) . Not used    ( 0) . Not used    ( 0) .
Antibiotic  8 . Not used    ( 0) . Not used    ( 0) . Not used    ( 0) .
Antibiotic  9 . Not used    ( 0) . Not used    ( 0) . Not used    ( 0) .
Antibiotic 10 . Trial 1     (32) . Trial 1     (32) . Trial 1     (32) .
Antibiotic 11 . Trial 2     (33) . Trial 2     (33) . Trial 2     (33) .
```

d) Enterobacteriaceae

```
Species name   .      E.coli        .    K.pneumoniae    .    Klebsiellae      .
Code 3 letter  .      eco           .    kpn             .    kle              .
Code 1 letter  .      e             .    k               .    K                .
Antibiotic  1 . Sulphonamide ( 1) . Sulphonamide ( 1) . Sulphonamide ( 1) .
Antibiotic  2 . Trimethoprim ( 2) . Trimethoprim ( 2) . Trimethoprim ( 2) .
Antibiotic  3 . Cotrimoxazol ( 3) . Cotrimoxazol ( 3) . Cotrimoxazol ( 3) .
Antibiotic  4 . Ampicillin   ( 4) . Ampicillin   ( 4) . Ampicillin   ( 4) .
Antibiotic  5 . Gentamicin   ( 5) . Gentamicin   ( 5) . Gentamicin   ( 5) .
Antibiotic  6 . Cefuroxime   ( 6) . Cefuroxime   ( 6) . Cefuroxime   ( 6) .
Antibiotic  7 . Nalidixate   ( 7) . Nalidixate   ( 7) . Nalidixate   ( 7) .
Antibiotic  8 . Nitrofurant  ( 8) . Nitrofurant  ( 8) . Nitrofurant  ( 8) .
Antibiotic  9 . Oral Ceph    ( 9) . Oral Ceph    ( 9) . Oral Ceph    ( 9) .
Antibiotic 10 . Trial 1      (32) . Trial 1      (32) . Trial 1      (32) .
Antibiotic 11 . Trial 2      (33) . Trial 2      (33) . Trial 2      (33) .


Species name   .    Enterobacter    .    Serratia        .    P.mirabilis      .
Code 3 letter  .      ent           .    ser             .    pmi              .
Code 1 letter  .      > (shift.)    .    < (shift,)      .    p                .
Antibiotic  1 . Sulphonamide ( 1) . Sulphonamide ( 1) . Sulphonamide ( 1) .
Antibiotic  2 . Trimethoprim ( 2) . Trimethoprim ( 2) . Trimethoprim ( 2) .
Antibiotic  3 . Cotrimoxazol ( 3) , Cotrimoxazol ( 3) . Cotrimoxazol ( 3) .
Antibiotic  4 . Ampicillin   ( 4) . Ampicillin   ( 4) . Ampicillin   ( 4) .
Antibiotic  5 . Gentamicin   ( 5) . Gentamicin   ( 5) . Gentamicin   ( 5) .
Antibiotic  6 . Cefuroxime   ( 6) . Cefuroxime   ( 6) . Cefuroxime   ( 6) .
Antibiotic  7 . Nalidixate   ( 7) . Nalidixate   ( 7) . Nalidixate   ( 7) .
Antibiotic  8 . Nitrofurant  ( 8) . Nitrofurant  ( 8) . Nitrofurant  ( 8) .
Antibiotic  9 . Oral Ceph    ( 9) . Oral Ceph    ( 9) . Oral Ceph    ( 9) .
Antibiotic 10 . Trial 1      (32) . Trial 1      (32) . Trial 1      (32) .
Antibiotic 11 . Trial 2      (33) . Trial 2      (33) . Trial 2      (33) .


Species name   .    P.vulgaris      .    P.morgani       .    P.rettgeri       .
Code 3 letter  .      pvu           .    pmo             .    pre              .
Code 1 letter  .      [             .    ]               .    (                .
Antibiotic  1 . Sulphonamide ( 1) . Sulphonamide ( 1) . Sulphonamide ( 1) .
Antibiotic  2 . Trimethoprim ( 2) . Trimethoprim ( 2) . Trimethoprim ( 2) .
Antibiotic  3 . Cotrimoxazol ( 3) . Cotrimoxazol ( 3) . Cotrimoxazol ( 3) .
Antibiotic  4 . Ampicillin   ( 4) . Ampicillin   ( 4) . Ampicillin   ( 4) .
Antibiotic  5 . Gentamicin   ( 5) . Gentamicin   ( 5) . Gentamicin   ( 5) .
Antibiotic  6 . Cefuroxime   ( 6) . Cefuroxime   ( 6) . Cefuroxime   ( 6) .
Antibiotic  7 . Nalidixate   ( 7) . Nalidixate   ( 7) . Nalidixate   ( 7) .
Antibiotic  8 . Nitrofurant  ( 8) . Nitrofurant  ( 8) . Nitrofurant  ( 8) .
Antibiotic  9 . Oral Ceph    ( 9) . Oral Ceph    ( 9) . Oral Ceph    ( 9) .
Antibiotic 10 . Trial 1      (32) . Trial 1      (32) . Trial 1      (32) .
Antibiotic 11 . Trial 2      (33) . Trial 2      (33) . Trial 2      (33) .
```

```
Species name    .    Providence      .   Citrobacter     .   Sh.sonnei           .
Code 3 letter   .    pro             .   cit             .   sso                 .
Code 1 letter   .    )               .   c               .   =                   .
Antibiotic  1   . Sulphonamide ( 1)  . Sulphonamide ( 1) . Sulphonamide ( 1)  .
Antibiotic  2   . Trimethoprim ( 2)  . Trimethoprim ( 2) . Trimethoprim ( 2)  .
Antibiotic  3   . Cotrimoxazol ( 3)  . Cotrimoxazol ( 3) . Cotrimoxazol ( 3)  .
Antibiotic  4   . Ampicillin   ( 4)  . Ampicillin   ( 4) . Ampicillin   ( 4)  .
Antibiotic  5   . Gentamicin   ( 5)  . Gentamicin   ( 5) . Gentamicin   ( 5)  .
Antibiotic  6   . Cefuroxime   ( 6)  . Cefuroxime   ( 6) . Cefuroxime   ( 6)  .
Antibiotic  7   . Nalidixate   ( 7)  . Nalidixate   ( 7) . Nalidixate   ( 7)  .
Antibiotic  8   . Nitrofurant  ( 8)  . Nitrofurant  ( 8) . Nitrofurant  ( 8)  .
Antibiotic  9   . Oral Ceph    ( 9)  . Oral Ceph    ( 9) . Oral Ceph    ( 9)  .
Antibiotic 10   . Trial 1      (32)  . Trial 1      (32) . Trial 1      (32)  .
Antibiotic 11   . Trial 2      (33)  . Trial 2      (33) . Trial 2      (33)  .


Species name    .    S.typhi         .   Salmonellae     .   Enteropath eco  .
Code 3 letter   .    sty             .   sal             .   eec             .
Code 1 letter   .    !               .   S               .   *               .
Antibiotic  1   . Sulphonamide ( 1)  . Sulphonamide ( 1) . Neomycin     (19) .
Antibiotic  2   . Trimethoprim ( 2)  . Trimethoprim ( 2) . Not used     ( 0) .
Antibiotic  3   . Cotrimoxazol ( 3)  . Cotrimoxazol ( 3) . Not used     ( 0) .
Antibiotic  4   . Ampicillin   ( 4)  . Ampicillin   ( 4) . Not used     ( 0) .
Antibiotic  5   . Gentamicin   ( 5)  . Gentamicin   ( 5) . Not used     ( 0) .
Antibiotic  6   . Chloramphen  (15)  . Chloramphen  (15) . Not used     ( 0) .
Antibiotic  7   . Not used     ( 0)  . Neomycin     (19) . Not used     ( 0) .
Antibiotic  8   . Not used     ( 0)  . Not used     ( 0) . Not used     ( 0) .
Antibiotic  9   . Not used     ( 0)  . Not used     ( 0) . Not used     ( 0) .
Antibiotic 10   . Trial 1      (32)  . Trial 1      (32) . Trial 1      (32) .
Antibiotic 11   . Trial 2      (33)  . Trial 2      (33) . Trial 2      (33) .
```

e) Other Gram Negative Bacilli

```
Species name    .    H.influenzae    .   Haemophilus     .   B.pertussis        .
Code 3 letter   .    hin             .   hae             .   bpe                .
Code 1 letter   .    h               .   H               .   o                  .
Antibiotic  1   . Sulphonamide ( 1)  . Sulphonamide ( 1) . Not used     ( 0)  .
Antibiotic  2   . Trimethoprim ( 2)  . Trimethoprim ( 2) . Not used     ( 0)  .
Antibiotic  3   . Cotrimoxazol ( 3)  . Cotrimoxazol ( 3) . Not used     ( 0)  .
Antibiotic  4   . Ampicillin   ( 4)  . Ampicillin   ( 4) . Not used     ( 0)  .
Antibiotic  5   . Erythromycin (12)  . Erythromycin (12) . Not used     ( 0)  .
Antibiotic  6   . Tetracycline (16)  . Tetracycline (16) . Not used     ( 0)  .
Antibiotic  7   . Chloramphen  (15)  . Chloramphen  (15) . Not used     ( 0)  .
Antibiotic  8   . Not used     ( 0)  . Not used     ( 0) . Not used     ( 0)  .
Antibiotic  9   . Not used     ( 0)  . Not used     ( 0) . Not used     ( 0)  .
Antibiotic 10   . Trial 1      (32)  . Trial 1      (32) . Trial 1      (32)  .
Antibiotic 11   . Trial 2      (33)  . Trial 2      (33) . Trial 2      (33)  .
```

```
Species name  .     Acinetobacter  .    Moraxella       .     Pasteurella        .
Code 3 letter .     aci            .    mor             .     pas                .
Code 1 letter .     7              .    m               .     t                  .
Antibiotic  1 . Sulphonamide ( 1) . Penicillin   (11) . Penicillin   (11) .
Antibiotic  2 . Trimethoprim ( 2) . Tetracycline (16) . Tetracycline (16) .
Antibiotic  3 . Cotrimoxazol ( 3) . Erythromycin (12) . Erythromycin (12) .
Antibiotic  4 . Ampicillin   ( 4) . Fluclox      (13) . Chloramphen  (15) .
Antibiotic  5 . Gentamicin   ( 5) . Not used     ( 0) . Not used     ( 0) .
Antibiotic  6 . Cefuroxime   ( 6) . Not used     ( 0) . Not used     ( 0) .
Antibiotic  7 . Nalidixate   ( 7) . Not used     ( 0) . Not used     ( 0) .
Antibiotic  8 . Nitrofurant  ( 8) . Not used     ( 0) . Not used     ( 0) .
Antibiotic  9 . Oral Ceph    ( 9) . Not used     ( 0) . Not used     ( 0) .
Antibiotic 10 . Trial 1      (32) . Trial 1      (32) . Trial 1      (32) .
Antibiotic 11 . Trial 2      (33) . Trial 2      (33) . Trial 2      (33) .


Species name  .     B.fragilis     .    Bacteroides     .    Fusobacteria      .
Code 3 letter .     bfr            .    bac             .    fus               .
Code 1 letter .     q              .    f               .    z                 .
Antibiotic  1 . Metrinidazol (22) . Metronidazol (22) . Metronidazol (22) .
Antibiotic  2 . Penicillin   (11) . Penicillin   (11) . Penicillin   (11) .
Antibiotic  3 . Clindamycin  (18) . Clindamycin  (18) . Clindamycin  (18) .
Antibiotic  4 . Not used     ( 0) . Not used     ( 0) . Not used     ( 0) .
Antibiotic  5 . Not used     ( 0) . Not used     ( 0) . Not used     ( 0) .
Antibiotic  6 . Not used     ( 0) . Not used     ( 0) . Not used     ( 0) .
Antibiotic  7 . Not used     ( 0) . Not used     ( 0) . Not used     ( 0) .
Antibiotic  8 . Not used     ( 0) . Not used     ( 0) . Not used     ( 0) .
Antibiotic  9 . Not used     ( 0) . Not used     ( 0) . Not used     ( 0) .
Antibiotic 10 . Trial 1      (32) . Trial 1      (32) . Trial 1      (32) .
Antibiotic 11 . Trial 2      (33) . Trial 2      (33) . Trial 2      (33) .


Species name  .     Ps.aeruginosa  .    Pseudomonas     .    Aeromonas          .
Code 3 letter .     pae            .    pse             .    aer                .
Code 1 letter .     y              .    u               .    r                  .
Antibiotic  1 . Gentamicin   ( 5) . Gentamicin   ( 5) . Sulphonamide ( 1) .
Antibiotic  2 . Tobramycin   (23) . Tobramycin   (23) . Trimethoprim ( 2) .
Antibiotic  3 . Piperacillin (24) . Piperacillin (24) . Cotrimoxazol ( 3) .
Antibiotic  4 . Colistin     (25) . Colistin     (25) . Ampicillin   ( 4) .
Antibiotic  5 . Not used     ( 0) . Not used     ( 0) . Gentamicin   ( 5) .
Antibiotic  6 . Not used     ( 0) . Not used     ( 0) . Cefuroxime   ( 6) .
Antibiotic  7 . Not used     ( 0) . Not used     ( 0) . Nalidixate   ( 7) .
Antibiotic  8 . Not used     ( 0) . Not used     ( 0) . Nitrofurant  ( 8) .
Antibiotic  9 . Not used     ( 0) . Not used     ( 0) . Oral Ceph    ( 9) .
Antibiotic 10 . Trial 1      (32) . Trial 1      (32) . Trial 1      (32) .
Antibiotic 11 . Trial 2      (33) . Trial 2      (33) . Trial 2      (33) .
```

f) Odds and ends

```
Species name   .  Campylobacter   .  Vibrio         .  Candida            .
Code 3 letter  .  cam             .  vib            .  can                .
Code 1 letter  .  v               .  V              .  Y                  .
Antibiotic  1  . Not used  ( 0) . Not used   ( 0) . Nystatin     (26) .
Antibiotic  2  . Not used  ( 0) . Not used   ( 0) . 5 F Cytosin  (28) .
Antibiotic  3  . Not used  ( 0) . Not used   ( 0) . Miconazole   (29) .
Antibiotic  4  . Not used  ( 0) . Not used   ( 0) . Amphotericin (27) .
Antibiotic  5  . Not used  ( 0) . Not used   ( 0) . Not used     ( 0) .
Antibiotic  6  . Not used  ( 0) . Not used   ( 0) . Not used     ( 0) .
Antibiotic  7  . Not used  ( 0) . Not used   ( 0) . Not used     ( 0) .
Antibiotic  8  . Not used  ( 0) . Not used   ( 0) . Not used     ( 0) .
Antibiotic  9  . Not used  ( 0) . Not used   ( 0) . Not used     ( 0) .
Antibiotic 10  . Trial 1   (32) . Trial 1    (32) . Trial 1      (32) .
Antibiotic 11  . Trial 2   (33) . Trial 2    (33) . Trial 2      (33) .
```

g) Parasites

```
Species name   .  Worms          .  Giardia        .  Amoebae          .
Code 3 letter  .  wor            .  gia            .  amo              .
Code 1 letter  .  w              .  g              .  b                .
Antibiotic  1  . Not used  ( 0) . Not used   ( 0) . Not used  ( 0) .
Antibiotic  2  . Not used  ( 0) . Not used   ( 0) . Not used  ( 0) .
Antibiotic  3  . Not used  ( 0) . Not used   ( 0) . Not used  ( 0) .
Antibiotic  4  . Not used  ( 0) . Not used   ( 0) . Not used  ( 0) .
Antibiotic  5  . Not used  ( 0) . Not used   ( 0) . Not used  ( 0) .
Antibiotic  6  . Not used  ( 0) . Not used   ( 0) . Not used  ( 0) .
Antibiotic  7  . Not used  ( 0) . Not used   ( 0) . Not used  ( 0) .
Antibiotic  8  . Not used  ( 0) . Not used   ( 0) . Not used  ( 0) .
Antibiotic  9  . Not used  ( 0) . Not used   ( 0) . Not used  ( 0) .
Antibiotic 10  . Not used  ( 0) . Not used   ( 0) . Not used  ( 0) .
Antibiotic 11  . Not used  ( 0) . Not used   ( 0) . Not used  ( 0) .
```

f) Viruses

```
Species name   .  Rotavirus      .  Adenovirus     .  Measles          .
Code 3 letter  .  rot            .  ade            .  mea              .
Code 1 letter  .  R              .  8              .  9                .
Antibiotic  1  . Not used  ( 0) . Not used   ( 0) . Not used  ( 0) .
Antibiotic  2  . Not used  ( 0) . Not used   ( 0) . Not used  ( 0) .
Antibiotic  3  . Not used  ( 0) . Not used   ( 0) . Not used  ( 0) .
Antibiotic  4  . Not used  ( 0) . Not used   ( 0) . Not used  ( 0) .
Antibiotic  5  . Not used  ( 0) . Not used   ( 0). Not used  ( 0) .
Antibiotic  6  . Not used  ( 0) . Not used   ( 0) . Not used  ( 0) .
Antibiotic  7  . Not used  ( 0) . Not used   ( 0) . Not used  ( 0) .
Antibiotic  8  . Not used  ( 0) . Not used   ( 0) . Not used  ( 0) .
Antibiotic  9  . Not used  ( 0) . Not used   ( 0) . Not used  ( 0) .
Antibiotic 10  . Not used  ( 0) . Not used   ( 0) . Not used  ( 0) .
Antibiotic 11  . Not used  ( 0) . Not used   ( 0) . Not used  ( 0) .
```

Species name	.	Mumps		.	Herpes		.	Varicella		.
Code 3 letter	.	mum		.	her		.	var		.
Code 1 letter	.	U		.	N		.	X		.
Antibiotic 1	. Not used	(0)	. Not used	(0)	. Not used	(0)	.
Antibiotic 2	. Not used	(0)	. Not used	(0)	. Not used	(0)	.
Antibiotic 3	. Not used	(0)	. Not used	(0)	. Not used	(0)	.
Antibiotic 4	. Not used	(0)	. Not used	(0)	. Not used	(0)	.
Antibiotic 5	. Not used	(0)	. Not used	(0)	. Not used	(0)	.
Antibiotic 6	. Not used	(0)	. Not used	(0)	. Not used	(0)	.
Antibiotic 7	. Not used	(0)	. Not used	(0)	. Not used	(0)	.
Antibiotic 8	. Not used	(0)	. Not used	(0)	. Not used	(0)	.
Antibiotic 9	. Not used	(0)	. Not used	(0)	. Not used	(0)	.
Antibiotic 10	. Not used	(0)	. Not used	(0)	. Not used	(0)	.
Antibiotic 11	. Not used	(0)	. Not used	(0)	. Not used	(0)	.

INDEX